National Pr[...]
Derek Fo[...]

"Thanks to a solid investment plan and a knack for picking the right stocks he (Derek Foster) was able to retire, mortgage-free, at age 34." — *ROBTV*

"Most Canadians work decades for the freedom Derek Foster has earned for his young family." — *Toronto Star*

"For Mr. Foster, 36, investing isn't about going for the quick score by gambling on a hot stock or sector." — *Globe and Mail*

"He's (Derek Foster) playing his very own game, which he's winning…" — *National Post*

"…— and he did it by turning the whole concept of what it means to save for retirement on its head." — *Moneysense (magazine)*

"While Warren Buffett is known as the oracle of Omaha, investment whiz Derek Foster could be labelled the Wise Man of Wasaga Beach." — *Toronto Sun*

The *Lazy* *Investor*

Start with $50... and
<u>no</u> Investment Knowledge

The no thinking strategy from
Canada's
Youngest Retiree

FOSTER, UNDERHILL FINANCIAL PRESS

Library and Archives Canada Cataloguing in Publication
Foster, Derek, 1970–
    The lazy investor: start with $50...
    and no investment knowledge/Derek Foster
ISBN 978-0-9736960-1-1
HG4521.F68 2007   332.6   C2007-904380-1

Published by
Foster, Underhill Financial Press
Suite 508, 900 Greenbank Road
Ottawa, ON Canada K2J 4P6

Phone toll free at: 1 888 686 STOP (1 888 686 7867)
or 613 823 2143
www.stopworking.ca

Design/formatting/production: WeMakeBooks.ca
Printed and bound in Canada

Legal Disclaimer

This book is intended to show you a strategy that you might want to consider for investing.

However, you must realize that I am not a professional with regard to any of the information I've provided in this book. I am merely presenting a strategy that I feel might be of interest to you. I am not an expert in economic, legal, taxation, investing, realty, or any other financial or related matters. The examples I provide are just that — examples. These are intended for illustrative purposes only. They are not an indication of what rate of return or future amount of money you might have if you followed the specific examples. They are only presented to illustrate the general concepts. Before initiating any of the strategies outlined, seek the advice of a competent professional to help you.

The book is intended as a general guide and should not be viewed as the ultimate source for financial information. Further research is needed and assistance must be sought from a qualified expert, before any action is taken by the reader. For further information, there is a recommended reading list at the back of this book. The information in these books might be incomplete, inaccurate, or out of date, so the reader should verify any of this information before acting on it.

Acknowledgements

Once again, there are some individuals I need to thank who offered their support. Written words fail to express my heartfelt appreciation.

First, I would like to thank my wife, Hyeeun. Caring for three kids while having another on the way is no easy task — one made more difficult by the many hours of work it took me to write this book. You came through again. Thank you!

To my Mom, Tina Colonnese, a special thank you once again for your input and double-checking my writing to make sure the ideas being conveyed were comprehensive, interesting, and to the point.

To my good friend, Stephane Lachapelle, thank you for taking the time to help me make sure the "whole thing made sense". Your input is greatly appreciated.

Finally, to my friend Todd Lavigne — thank you for showing me that I am indeed, "the lazy investor", and encouraging me to put that right on the cover of the book.

Thank you.

TABLE OF CONTENTS

"What we see depends mainly on what we look for."

■ **Sir John Lubbock**

1

WHY DO THE RICH ALWAYS GET RICHER?

*"If hard work were such a wonderful thing,
surely the rich would have kept it all to themselves."*

■ **Lane Kirkland**

Why is it that the people who have money tend to get richer whereas the regular working class keep at a standstill? The basic answer boils down to this — working for a living is *not* the road to riches! Having *your money work for you* is the key to building wealth.

You've heard the standard dogma for success, "Get a good education, work hard, and you'll be successful." It's a good start — but it's only *part* of the equation. There are other actions that can help you gain financial freedom without taking on a lot of risk or making a huge time commitment.

The entire financial industry has been built up to help people become wealthy. Banks, stock brokers, and mutual fund companies are places where average people can go to invest and build their wealth. But how many rich people use these products and services? Are these really great wealth creation vehicles or are they a poor substitute for what real wealthy individuals invest in? How much do the various fees they charge eat into the profits?

I do know that people who *own* financial companies have done very well for themselves! I own some bank shares and have been very happy. I'm pleased when I see the notices go out announcing another round of fee increases. These increases simply mean that the bank should be in the position to make more money and raise its dividend — the money it pays to shareholders! These dividends have risen substantially over time.

Basically, this is the key to wealth creation — be an owner. Let's use a typical blue-chip company (a bank for example) to look at this a little further. "Blue-chip" generally refers to companies that are very stable and have long operating histories.

Banks make money from mortgages, credit cards, wealth management fees, and a variety of other areas. This is where the profit comes from. Suppose your company earns $1 per share in profit. Usually around 40 cents of that amount is paid out in dividends (cheques sent to shareholders) and the other 60 cents is reinvested. This reinvestment creates *increased* profits, so the next year instead of earning only $1 per share, the bank might now earn $1.10. Now, perhaps 44 cents of the *new higher* profit is paid out to shareholders, while 66 cents is retained and reinvested. This happens year after year, with greater amounts being reinvested over time (and also larger dividends being paid). That's why the rich get richer — a large part of their wealth is continually reinvested — automatically!

Furthermore, rich families stay rich by passing on their wealth through the generations. Most of us have been taught to seek out a stable job with good benefits and a pension plan. This can be a great starting point but investing is the key to real wealth creation. Your pension mostly "disappears" after you and your spouse have passed on, whereas real wealth keeps on flowing onto successive generations. That's the reason why the rich *stay* rich and the rest of us keep on working but never get ahead — they focus on *real* wealth!

Once again, these are the key factors — be an owner and reinvest! That's going to be the simple focus of this book. But really, this point is nothing new — you already know that.

The strategy in this book will highlight a different approach that's not widely advertised. I'm not a financial planner or an "expert", but my investment strategy has worked well enough that three years ago I retired — at the age of 34.

The prospect of the never-ending treadmill where there's no end except a far off promise of a pension didn't appeal to me so I created a simple strategy that led to my early exit from the work world. This strategy contradicted a lot of conventional wisdom — but who cares? I kept running into people in their 50s and 60s working in the financial industry telling me how I should invest for retirement. I kept asking myself, "If you're so great at investing, why are you still working in the industry instead of sipping margaritas by the ocean someplace warm?" Simply put, following conventional "wisdom" will lead you to achieving conventional results. I followed an *unconventional approach* and it created *unconventional results*.

Many people contacted me with their thoughts after learning about my strategy. Some people felt they didn't know enough about how to invest successfully while others didn't know how to start. Many people told me they didn't have the money. Others didn't know when a good time to buy stocks would be — when were they selling cheaply? How could they analyze them?

This book aims to address these questions and resolve them for you. It will give you an actual list of securities you can invest in. You can start with a very small amount of money and without any investment knowledge — mechanically following the strategy without any thought or research. You won't have to analyze companies to decide when it's a good time to buy. You won't have to pay large fees which enrich everyone else — but you! You simply start the strategy and set it on autopilot! A virtual roadmap explaining how to accomplish all this will be covered in the first section of the book. This is how I would go about investing if I was starting all over again. This is the strategy I am following to get my own children started in investing. It's a strategy for beginners.

The second section offers ideas on how to teach money-related issues to children (or grandchildren). It will show you how to implement the investment strategy mentioned above for children and get them started early. The appendix will answer some of the questions many readers of my first book have asked.

Enjoy!

SECTION I

Achieving Financial Freedom —
(Your Roadmap)

2

IF YOU WANT SOMETHING DONE RIGHT, DO IT YOURSELF!

"A stockbroker is someone who invests other people's money until it's all gone."

▥ **Woody Allen**

I have to emphasize this — if you want to reach financial freedom for you and your family, the best way is to do it *yourself*. I know we are inundated with TV commercials explaining how hard it is to invest and how you should simply hand your money over to the professionals to manage. Let's face it — investing can be a daunting challenge. But what about the costs to you? How much do they add up to?

Let's take your typical mutual fund and compare. If you were to invest $100,000 for 25 years in a portfolio of stocks and they averaged 10% per year, you would end up with **$1,083,000**.

If you put a mutual fund bureaucracy between you and your stock ownership and the annual expenses of the funds were 2%, then your return would be reduced to 8% per year (10%–2%). Your total investment would then amount to only **$685,000**.

The difference is over **$400,000** *or almost 40% less money with a 2% fee!* Many funds have expense ratios much higher than 2%.

With enough people investing and paying fees, you can see why there are so many luxury cars being driven around Bay Street (the home of the financial industry in Canada). When you look at a wealth accumulation situation, there are three scenarios — a negative sum game, a positive sum game, or a zero sum game.

A negative sum game is where for every dollar put in, only a fraction of it comes back — a lottery ticket would be a good example. When all the money is put in, the lottery ticket organizer takes its share and the rest is paid out — a terrible deal for ticket buyers!

A zero sum game would be poker night with your friends. Everyone contributes to the pot, but there is no entity taking a cut off the top — money is simply shuffled around from player to player. Some players might be better and win more often, but the total of all the players' money remains the same.

Investing is a positive sum game. Companies grow over time and there's more wealth available. For example, one share of Coca-Cola worth $40 in 1919 when the company went public would have been worth almost $2 million by 1991 with reinvested dividends — and that original share is worth even more today!

The negative-sum games are great for the owners —
which is why various governments usually have a monop-
oly on these activities. Lottery tickets and casinos (huge
money-makers) are owned by various governments in
Canada. As an interesting note, governments also tax
addictive products (tobacco, alcohol) quite heavily
because direct ownership would be frowned upon but
high taxation gives the same effect. If there wasn't this
high taxation, the companies themselves would raise their
prices to maximize their profits. In the US, many states
were successful at extracting money from tobacco companies to pay for medical costs to treat sick smokers with a
settlement signed in 1998 worth over $200 billion over 25
years. The perverse result is that the states' interest in col-
lecting this money is dependent on the continued existence of the big tobacco companies.

Since private companies can't own most of the negative-sum games, they take the positive sum games and take
a "cut". Therefore, the great growth of the stock market
can be harnessed. By using other people's money (maybe
yours), the financial industry can earn a good profit without taking on a lot of risk. If your fund manager chooses
stocks that go down — *you* lose money, but the fund company doesn't — and they still collect their fees.

Many people ignore investment fees thinking they
don't pay any. For example, I've heard the comment, "Oh,
I'm in no-load funds". This simply means you don't pay
an *initial* fee to enter into the arrangement. However,

management fees are taken from the funds every year —
you just don't *notice* it. You're not sent a bill or anything
like that — they just collect the management fees off the
top. This is the exact same way the government collects
income tax from your paycheque. As mentioned above,
they still get their fees even if you lose money — sort of
win-win, for them — without assuming the risk.

I think the way this system is designed is unfair to the
people investing their money. Currently the fund companies make a percentage of the total assets under their management — regardless of how they perform. So if the
portfolio loses money in any year — the fund company still
makes money. This system seems perverse. I like the
method Warren Buffett used when he managed money
through a partnership. Basically he earned a quarter of all
profits over a 6% rate of return. So if the portfolio made
anything less than 6%, Buffett made absolutely nothing,
but he earned 25 cents out of every dollar of profits above
the 6% rate of return.

This system rewards outperformance but doesn't
charge investors for underperformance (or losses). If you
make a good rate of return, so does the money manager.
Your interests are more aligned. It would be much fairer
for fund companies to earn a much *larger* percentage, but
only on results above a certain benchmark (like the system
above). Since the system doesn't work this way, I'm not
interested in participating — except perhaps by owning
shares in the financial companies selling these products.

In discussing my original strategy I argued that the best way to go about investing was to open up a discount brokerage account and buy quality, recession-proof stocks and simply sit and collect the dividends. I still advocate this approach as it has served me very well. Since retiring three years ago my income has kept increasing as these wonderful companies raise their dividends (the money they send to shareholders).

However, many people are reluctant to buy shares directly. They don't have a lot of background in investing so they question how they could invest as well as the professionals.

I'm going to explain a few of the advantages that small investors *do* have. For starters, small investors have one main goal — to make a decent return on their money. Sure, mutual fund companies might have the same goal, but there is one thing many managers care more about — keeping their job! If the stock markets go into a euphoric frenzy and people are bidding up the price of a stock or a sector of stocks to unrealistic levels, many funds automatically follow along so they don't get left behind.

Let me give you a real-life example. We'll use the "tech bubble" of the late 1990s (where hi-tech stocks were selling for ridiculous prices) to illustrate. Let's highlight a stock that was the media darling at that time — Nortel. During this time, shares of Nortel were flying high — to unsustainable levels. There was a general euphoria surrounding the market and tech stocks were the place to be!

If any fund manager avoided this sector because the stocks were too expensive, their performance would trail badly — at least in the short-term. In order to make sure they at least kept pace with their peers, many fund managers had to make sure they had some exposure to stocks like Nortel — or else they could find themselves out of a job. They bought the stock everyone had to own — even if it was overpriced at that level. Longer-term investors would have been better served if the managers of their mutual funds had avoided Nortel (and luckily some did), but many fund managers did not and their investors got crushed and paid for this poor decision.

The stock reached a peak of $124/share and then started its long descent — all the way down to 47 cents. To put this dismal performance into perspective, I heard a humorous comparison. If an investor had instead bought beer and returned the empty bottles, he would have been better off than if he had put his money into this stock at its zenith.

The other factor which mutual funds have going against their performance is that there are many small investors and the funds must adapt to the behaviour of these investors. It's interesting to note that mutual fund sales are widely seen as a contrary indicator for the market. Let me explain what this means.

Although the long-term trend of the market is up, over shorter periods of time the market moves in cycles — either "bull" or "bear" markets. A bull market is when prices are moving higher, while a bear market is one in which prices are moving down. After a bear market, prices are depressed and every headline in the financial media is negative — there's simply nothing positive to see in the market.

When pessimism abounds, "value" investors (those looking for under priced stocks) move in trying to find bargain stocks that are selling cheaply. Tentatively, they stick their toes into the market waters. Slowly they start buying shares — which causes the share prices to rise.

As this happens, a few more investors start seeing silver linings amongst all the storm clouds and they put their money into the market, further driving up prices. Gradually more and more people buy stocks and the whole process feeds on itself.

Finally everyone is making money on stocks. There are blue skies and sunshine over the entire market. Your neighbours are making money in stocks — heck even your neighbour's dog is making money! A sort of buying panic ensues as people scramble into the markets to buy — not wanting to miss the gravy train. Usually the last people to invest in the market are novice investors, who throw their money into mutual funds. Fund sales go through the roof and the fund managers scramble to put all that money to work. But at this stage the euphoria is unjustified — usually around the time mutual fund sales peak. This stage is often followed by another bear market and many of the novice investors lose money. That's why mutual fund sales are often seen as a contrary indicator:

When mutual fund sales soar, often the stock market is at its peak and about to decline.

The investors who make the most money are those who come to the party early. Those who arrive late just end up with half-empty beer bottles and half-eaten cold pizza. A quote from Robert Kiyosaki (author of *"Rich Dad, Poor Dad"*) explains this:

"When dumb money chases smart money, the party's over."

The best investor in the world is Warren Buffett. I follow what he has to say because he has a proven track record — and over $40 billion. I don't care if thousands of people who make their money by *selling* investments contradict this one person who makes his money by *owning* investments. His approach is summarized in the quote:

"Investors should remember that excitement and expenses are their enemies. And if they insist on trying to time their participation in equities, they should try to be fearful when others are greedy and greedy when others are fearful."

Mutual funds work the opposite way — they pile money into the market much closer to the top than the bottom. It's interesting to note that in many years 80% or more of mutual funds don't perform as well as the market. Think about it — sophisticated managers earning large salaries with well-developed research at their disposal — and the vast majority can't keep up with the market! It's also interesting to note that a lot of fund investors don't do as well as the funds themselves because they add money to the fund *after* it's had a great run.

Notice the above quote mentions, "...*if they insist on trying to time their participation....*" Simply put, it's better to buy and hold — act like a real *owner* and don't worry about the manic-depressive behaviour of the stock market!

If mutual funds might not work, how about getting advice from a broker? You could, but there are drawbacks here as well.

First, one of the ways many brokers earn their money is from commissions — when investors buy or sell stocks. They make more money when people trade often. But once again, many of the most successful investors argue that a buy and hold approach is better for achieving wealth. Every time you sell a stock, there are commissions to pay (and also capital gains taxes). In this case, your goal and that of your broker might be different.

Are there any other potential problems? Another area of concern is to do with underwriting — which is simply when firms sell their stocks or bonds to investors to raise money. In a paper entitled, "Policy Remedies for Conflicts of Interest in the Financial System" by Frederic Mishkin (I understand it might not be your regular bedtime reading), the author makes a point that "Issuers (companies selling shares to the public) benefit from optimistic research, while investors desire unbiased research." In other words, there might be an incentive for analysts working for larger bro-kerages to say a certain stock looks great, when in reality it doesn't. This rosy forecast might help bring in underwriting business and make the brokerage more money — but it doesn't help small investors.

The point of all this is not to say that everyone in the financial industry is "out to get you". It demonstrates that their incentives are not perfectly aligned with yours. There are a lot of good, honest people (and companies) operating in this industry, but you should be aware of possible pitfalls. If you are a minnow swimming with the sharks, it's best to know where the sharks eat — so you avoid that area and protect yourself.

I love the stock market and investing in stocks — but I am definitely a "minnow". A lot of people don't have the time or interest to follow investments — and these are the people this book was written for. Here you will use an automatic investment approach where you won't have to think — where your emotions won't enter the equation and be able to work against you. With this system you will automatically buy more shares when markets are low and buy fewer when markets are high. You will also avoid two of the enemies of wealth accumulation, "excitement and expenses" as mentioned above. This investing method is so boring — it's robotic in nature. It also avoids many of the expenses the novice investor often faces when having to pay others to manage their money.

Finally, it's going to address an important reality would-be investors face. Many people don't have a large sum of money ready to invest immediately. In revealing my original investment strategy, I explained how to build a port-folio if you *already* had some money to invest. Mutual funds offer a solution to those who want to contribute a small amount of money every month but there are fees to pay. The strategy in this book will help you avoid these costs. In the example at the beginning of this chapter, these fees resulted in the investor earning 40% less money. Discount brokerage accounts for direct stock purchases don't work because if you're only contributing a small amount every month, commissions would eat up a substantial portion of the money you wanted to invest. That's why this book will show you how to gradually build up your own portfolio without having your pockets emptied with fees. Please don't mention this to anyone you pay fees to in the financial industry. It's not illegal or anything — but I would hate to send all the "BMW Bankers" and "Mercedes Mutual Funders" into conniptions.

3

SCHOOL DAZE, FINANCIAL MAZE — IT'S ALL A HAZE

"If Calculus or Algebra were required to be a great investor, I'd have to go back to delivering newspapers."

■ **Warren Buffett** (Billionaire Investor)

In my opinion, a lot of what people learn about investing is misguided or just plain wrong. Let's take a moment to examine why.

First, the school system ignores it. I was educated in Ontario, where at that time the school system went up to grade 13 (the only place I'm aware of where this was the case). I also had attended Junior and Senior Kindergarten. So prior to attending university, I had received 15 years of formal education. I learned Shakespeare, Calculus, World Geography, Drama, History… and a load of other subjects — some useful, some of questionable value. However, during all that time I had never once been offered a personal finance course.

Think about this for a moment. One of the life skills that virtually every person needs to function in society was never covered. How does one buy a house? What are CMHC fees and how can you avoid them? Why are credit cards flogged so openly on university campuses? Why does indebtedness essentially make you a wage slave? Why does the stock market exist and how can its existence help you achieve your financial dreams? How do you balance a cheque book? I'm not saying money is the most important thing, but a basic financial course would be an asset. I agree with Clinton Jones when he said, "I have never been in a situation where having money made it worse."

Schools are good for teaching you how to get a career — but they don't teach you how to achieve financial freedom. You have to find a way to learn this for yourself!

Only one high school course covered the topic of the stock market. One of my favourite teachers (my grade 13 Economics teacher), created a simulated stock market game where we could take a fictitious $100,000 and invest it in the stock market. The results were tracked over the course of three months and the group with the most "money" were the winners.

It was a good attempt, but of limited value. The time frame was much too short which allowed the speculators who took on major risks to win. This is totally the wrong message that should be sent. This is the main weakness in most stock market contests I've seen — they're simply another form of gambling. I would venture to say that even the best investors in the world would not have an advantage in this short-term casino mentality type of contest. You're betting on a quick spin of the wheel, and hoping to strike it rich — even if it's only imaginary money!

Another fact that bothers me in retrospect was that my teacher explained how he had created this contest to show how hard it is to make money in the stock market. Of course it's hard to make money over a three month period, but a quick look at the Forbes list of world's richest people shows that most of them have significant shareholdings — mostly in their own companies. This is why I advocate "buy and hold" as the cornerstone of my investing strategy. Investors have to move as close as possible to being real owners of a business *rather than traders* of stocks.

> *The stock market is the greatest wealth creation device ever invented — but you have to do it right. It's not a short-term, casino-like entity. It's a place to participate in the long-term success of the companies that provide the goods and services all of us need everyday!*

Additionally, I've found over the years that proper investing is only 10% intellectual and 90% emotional. Some people watch the stock market daily and their emotions rise and fall with its performance. Once you put your own hard-earned money into stocks it's much different than simply choosing ticker symbols and "investing" non-existent dollars. This exercise totally ignored the emotional aspect of investing — which is the most important part.

You don't have to be all that smart to be a successful investor. For some perverse reason, people prefer complex answers to simple problems. Invest in simple businesses, don't sweat the small stuff and your returns will be quite satisfactory!

The final reason I didn't like this approach was a quick chat we had while in Montreal. The class had taken a field trip to the Montreal Stock Exchange and visited a brokerage house. I vividly remember asking my teacher if he owned any stocks. He replied that he had never owned any. I question how one can properly teach about something they've never directly participated in? I feel it is better to learn from people who have actually done what you are trying to learn to do.

A lot of the advice about stocks and investing are given by people who don't have much experience themselves — or only bad experiences. I've found behind bad investing experiences there usually lays bad investing strategies.

Now his reluctance to buy stocks was not illogical — in fact this approach made sense for someone in his position. He had a union job with a comfortable income where he was sheltered from downturns in the economy. He also had a very stable and secure pension. Essentially, as long as he kept doing his job, he could gradually pay down his mortgage and then spend every last cent he earned every paycheque and keep working until his pension kicked in and then he could take things easy. Why would he want to take any risk in the stock market? It didn't make any sense for him. But that is also why he was not the ideal person to teach about investing.

This example is not meant as an attack on teachers. As stated earlier, this fellow was one of my favourite teachers. His lessons were interesting; he presented them well, and was great at explaining his points. He simply had limited experience in investing and therefore was not the person to be teaching it. The idea of finding a well-paying, stable career where you're unlikely to be laid off with a great pension plan is an excellent strategy. The only trouble is that many people will never be in this type of situation. The pool of careers offering great pension plans is shrinking. The world is changing. This is why the school system has been of limited value for teaching financial information.

So where do people get the knowledge they need to invest? I've found a lot of them look to the financial industry for some insight. Banks, insurance companies, mutual fund companies, and brokerage houses with their highly paid stock analysts offer such information. This is where I started on my quest to learn about investing. The problem as mentioned earlier is that the goals of the financial industry are not totally congruent to mine (or yours), and this makes me question whether the advice offered serves our interests, or theirs.

Look at the example of a regular bank account. We've been taught the value of saving some money (a good thing), but then a lot of this money ends up in savings accounts (not a good thing). Banks offer accounts that are guaranteed by the Canada Deposit Insurance Corporation (CDIC) which is a federal crown corporation created by Parliament and insures accounts for up to $100,000. This means that if your bank is a member of CDIC and it fails, you're protected for amounts up to this threshold (you can go to the CDIC website for more information). The trouble with bank accounts is that they pay out very little in the way of interest. A quick check at one of the major banks reveals that you can garner between 0.1% for a daily interest savings account to a whopping 3% for a "high" interest savings account. The only caveat with the high interest account is that there is a $5 charge for withdrawing money from it but apparently there are certain ways to avoid this charge. Regardless, with the 3% return, you're hardly keeping up with inflation. If you add the fact that this interest is taxed, you'll be losing ground. This financial model in which parents bring their kids into the bank to save their money is simply locking them into the "Slave and Save" model without a chance for any real financial freedom down the road.

The next level offered is the ever-popular GICs (guaranteed investment certificates). A quick search on the internet at Investopedia mentions that a bank's profit is the difference between GIC rates and mortgage rates. I assume this was written before bank fees became so common, but it offers a good illustration. Here you're locking your money into a product for a certain period of time (usually 1-5 years). The rates offered by one of the banks I checked at the time of this writing range from 3% for a one-year term to slightly more than 4% for locking in your money at the bank for 5 years. These are not great rates of return. Nonetheless, the banks offer all sorts of information about these products — eager to sell them to you. Here's a tip I'd like to offer:

> *"Don't buy the banks' crummy products — wherever possible buy the banks' stock instead!"*

At the time of this writing, I can buy the stock of the exact bank that offered the products above (Scotiabank) with a dividend yield of 3.25%. In other words, if you buy bank shares instead of depositing money with the bank, you can get 3.25% on your money. This beats the highest interest savings account it offers and is competitive with the GIC rate. In addition, dividend income attracts a much lower rate of tax than interest income.

So bank *shares* rather than bank *products* is the place where you should consider directing your savings. The 3.25% dividend does not sound like much, but let's take a look at what has happened over the longer term. Time is a major factor in making money grow, so a small investment compounded over a long period of time can yield enormous results. For example, if you had invested in this bank on September 1, 1989 (when I started university), each share would have cost $18.38/share and would have paid a dividend of 88 cents or 4.8%. But every year as the bank made more money, it hiked its dividend. Here your goals are congruent to the people controlling the company. The directors, CEO, and others all have a large stake in how well the bank does, so they are motivated to make the bank do well

— and small investors can tag along for the ride! Here's a table to show how the dividend has risen over time:

YEAR	DIVIDEND/SHARE
1989	$0.88
1990	$1.00
1991	$1.00
1992	$1.04
1993	$1.12
1994	$1.16
1995	$1.24
1996	$1.30
1997	$1.48
1998	**2for1 stock split**
1999	$1.74
2000	$2.00
2001	$2.48
2002	$2.90
2003	$3.36
2004	**2for1 stock dividend**
2005	$5.28
2006	$6.00
2007	$6.72 (projected)

Note A 2for1 split or stock dividend will result in having 2 shares for every one share you originally owned. So if you had 1 share worth $100, and the stock splits 2for1, you now have 2 shares worth $50 each. The above table takes into account these stock splits.

The dividend has risen consistently so that with all the dividend hikes, the current dividend rate is equivalent to $6.72 on your original share. In other words, you would now be earning over 36% *every year* on your original investment if you had purchased shares in 1989! That dwarfs the tiny returns offered by even the most generous GICs. Remember, that's just the annual dividend and it ignores the capital gains that have also accrued to shareholders.

My strategy focuses on regular dividend payments, but it's interesting to note from the chart above that the shares of this company have split twice since 1989. Share splits occur when a company's share price has risen. Over time, great companies will become more and more valuable and this will be reflected in the share price. So if you pay $50/share but the company keeps growing, eventually the price might be $100/share, then $200/share, ... If the price never splits, the share price becomes so large that the average person can't buy any shares. For example, Berkshire Hathaway (a holding company in the US) hasn't had any share splits for decades. If you wanted to buy one of the original shares today, you'd have to come up with over $100,000 US! Getting back to the bank I mentioned above, for each share you bought in 1989, you'd now have 4 shares.

For a longer term comparison, suppose your grandfather or great-grandfather had bought only 10 shares at the beginning of 1944 — do you know how many shares that would amount to? The stock has split six times since then, and the total would have grown to 12,000 shares! So a small invest-ment combined with a lot of time yields BIG results.

SMALL amounts of money invested in great companies for long periods of time create very LARGE amounts of money!

How "safe" are these dividends? There are no guaran-tees that these will be paid, so do you really want to risk your money on something so risky?

Perhaps this is true, but this bank has paid dividends for longer than anyone in Canada has been alive. In fact, it's paid dividends continuously since 1833 (before Canada became a country). Over time the dividend payments grew substantially. This growth is a key factor we'll rely on in creating financial freedom for you. We'll cover how you can get your money invested in this and other investments — starting with small amounts.

But why buy the stocks directly? Why not get a pro-fessional mutual fund manager who can select the best stocks for you so you can just systematically put money into the fund and relax? A lot of what people have learned about investing has come from the mutual fund companies through various forms of advertising. The trouble I have is that once again, their goals are not entirely the same.

For example, people have been told that Canada rep-resents only 3% of the world economy so one should invest globally. Of course, for the individual, investing outside of North America is difficult to do — so the *con-venient answer* is to buy a fund that does it for you. I don't agree with this. A quick look at the richest people reveal that they have most of their wealth tied up in only one country. In fact, their money is usually invested in a *single* company — usually their own. If the mutual fund route is the way to go, why do the richest people invest the majority of their money in direct ownership of a company in their home country? Wouldn't it therefore make sense to act as much like an "owner" of a company by buying shares and then holding them for a very long time?

Another fact that I mentioned in the last chapter is that the vast majority of mutual funds underperform the market. By buying funds, you've essentially created a bureaucracy between you and your investment holdings. Every commercial you see on TV, the literature you're sent in the mail, the fees your advisor makes, the fancy high-rise offices in downtown Toronto — all of it comes out of the fees you pay! Of course, we're given the impression that these managers have certain knowledge that we don't have, so if we were to try and invest on our own, we'd be in trouble. Their insight will guide our portfolio through the rough patches and offer a chance to buy shares while they're a good value. Let's examine this for a moment. A quick search of dividend mutual funds in Canada shows that they charge between 1.00–2.5% a year. If you look at their top holdings, there's not much difference — they all invest in big banks, insurers, and a few others. With the example of the bank stock above with a 3.25% dividend being paid right now, the fees will eat up from one third to over two thirds of your dividend income! That's a huge amount. These fund managers have to outperform by a pretty large margin in order to overcome these costs — and the truth is that most of them fail to do so. Why do we rely so heavily on learning about investing through financial companies? Are their "teachings" provided for our benefit or for theirs?

If you want to create wealth, try to emulate what other wealthy individuals have done instead of listening to those who accumulate their own wealth by selling you investment products!

I never had anyone sit down and teach me about investing. Neither of my parents ever bought stocks before I did, so I had to learn it all on my own. I opened the typical savings account as a kid, but I started learning about investing around the time I started university. I had an interest so I studied business, but since that time I've had to "unlearn" a lot of what business school teaches. A lot of what is taught in finance, such as "efficient market hypothesis" (a complicated theory that is not worth a lot of time to go over here), is rejected by the best investors.

You don't need a special education to be a successful investor!

The way to learn about obtaining financial success is to study others who have already achieved it. I've read many financial books but eventually focused on the lessons of a few great investors as a guide. I used their ideas and applied their thinking to a Canadian perspective and added some of my own ideas.

I'm going to get into the nuts and bolts of this investment strategy over the next few chapters — but first I would like to explain why many people view stocks as being risky and how reality can be different. Once we've gone over that, the basic foundation for creating financial independence for you will incorporate the idea of buying solid companies. I'll explain how you can gradually buy small amounts of these companies over time without worrying about the state of the stock market. There will be no complex theories or calculations — just a common sense, simple approach!

4

LOTTERY TICKETS, CASINOS AND STOCKS!

"Lottery tickets are a tax on people who are poor at math"

■ **Unknown**

A quick check of the internet found that 18.9 million adult Canadians spent $11.3 billion on various forms of gambling in 2002. That equates to approximately $600 per person. In addition, this amount has grown from only $2.7 billion a decade ago — so it's quadrupled in ten years.

I am not a gambler. I have never bought a lottery ticket in my life. Mathematically, the odds are stacked against you so it's a "sucker's" bet. However, every time the Lotto 6/49 jackpot climbs, I'm amazed at how many people start lining up to buy tickets. This behaviour is something I can't understand.

I admit I did try my luck at a casino once. In 1980 my dad won a trip to Las Vegas and told me how he had spent some time playing Blackjack — and how he had become enamoured with the whole experience. He then followed that up with a trip to Atlantic City in the late 1980's. He claimed he had developed an iron-clad "system" whereby he could gradually win money over time. He told me how he had been "up" almost $2,000 at one point, but then he had deviated from his strategy and left the casino "even". I was intrigued, so I convinced him to go on one of the "free" trips he had been offered to Atlantic City and take me. I had just turned 21. It was incredible! There was a chauffer-driven Limo that picked us up and took us to the hotel. The room was opulent and offered an all-you-can-eat buffet which was free! I guess this was the lifestyle of all the "high rollers like us" — the rich people!

Upon arrival I decided to head down to the casino and look around. There were rows of slot machines and poker, blackjack and roulette tables. I settled on roulette and sat down to give it a try. I had brought a little more than $250 and had set that as a limit and if I lost it, I would not gamble anymore. In the back of my mind I envisioned perhaps coming back home with a tidy sum. I had decided to bet only colours (red or black) and to go to the cheapest table — a $2 minimum bet. My plan was to keep betting $2 as long as I won. If I lost, I would double my bet to win back what I had lost. I would keep doubling the bets until I won once and then my bet would be lowered back to $2.

If you have never played roulette before, in the US (the European tables are slightly different), there are 38 spaces on the roulette wheel — 18 black, 18 red, and two green. A little white marble is set in motion and the roulette wheel is spun in the opposite direction. By betting on either red or black, you have an 18/38 = 47% chance of winning and a 47% chance of losing (if it lands on the opposite colour). If it lands on one of the two green spots, you lose only half your bet. The table I chose had a $2 minimum bet and a $200 maximum bet — so if I kept losing, I would keep doubling my bets. If I lost a series of bets, the amounts wagered would keep increasing like this — $2,4,8,16,32,64,128. If I won any of those bets, my next bet would be reduced to the original $2. By my calculations, if I had an approximately 50% chance of winning, then the likelihood of losing 7 bets in a row would be around 1%. In other words, it would almost never happen with such a random game!

I confidently walked up to the table and placed my bet. For the first 20 minutes I was winning! It was exhilarating! My chip pile was growing! Then I encountered that 1 in a 100 streak and proceeded to lose my entire pile in about 10 minutes. I have to say that gambling is much more fun when you're winning than when you're losing. I now had a decision to make — what to do with the rest of the weekend.

There were many places that offered cash on your credit card and bank cards but I didn't take out any more. I had enrolled in a $250 course and had done very well. I had learned to never engage in any activity where the odds are stacked against you. Those 10 minutes of intense pain had taught me this valuable lesson.

The rest of the weekend was incredibly boring. I just wandered around without much to do — which allowed me to keep absorbing the lesson. Around the hotel I talked to many people and was surprised to find that virtually everyone was "up" (had won more money than they had lost). It seems *everyone* I spoke to had won money that weekend — a curious fact since casinos need people to lose money to stay in business. I've come to the conclusion that most gamblers are either liars or suffer from severe amnesia.

Gambling is poverty inducing — not a road to riches. The only ones who get rich with games of chance are the owners of the game!

So on to the stock market — is this gambling or what? I think the stock market has gotten a bad rap. As far as creating the potential for financial freedom, the stock market is a wonderful tool. The adage of never investing money you can't afford to lose is somewhat misguided. By not investing in the companies that produce the goods and services you use every day, you're missing an incredible opportunity. The younger the participant, the greater the opportunity! I'm sure more money has been lost because it remained in "safe" GICs than has been lost in stock market crashes.

The key is using the stock market correctly. Many people view the market as a get-rich-quick device and approach it in casino-like fashion. They place wagers on companies that have no earnings history or invest in industries that are deemed to be the "next hot thing". In most cases they lose their investments and then argue that the stock market is the same as gambling and should be avoided. In my first investment in Radio Shack where I worked part-time during university, I lost half my net worth. I too rejected the stock market as simply another casino. But gradually I came to realize that it was not the fault of the stock market that had cost me so much, but my own stupidity. After reading about the great investors who had become quite wealthy through investing, I came to realize that if one invests correctly (by following the ideas of those who have been successful), the results should be better!

If you treat the stock market like a casino, you'll end up with casino-like returns. If you treat the stock market like a partial ownership in great companies, you'll have owner-like returns. There are many company owners on the Forbes list of richest people! How many gamblers are on this list?

Investing the correct way is key! Just as you buy cows to get milk or hens to get eggs, you should buy stocks to get dividends. This changes your perspective. When the stock market goes down, then you can buy that stream of dividends for a cheaper price — it's a good thing! This important fact was the cornerstone for me being able to stop relying on a regular paycheque at such a young age. This is the factor that will start you on your road to financial freedom. The next chapter will tell you how.

5

MAKING WEALTH ACCUMULATION.... AUTOMATIC! THE SECRET "CULT"

"Most people are too busy earning a living to make any money"

■ **Anonymous**

I am a huge fan of the show *The Simpsons* and really think their writers are amazing. I remember one episode where Homer sees some co-workers who seem to be getting all sorts of "perks". They have great parking spots, free access to vending machines, and super-comfy chairs at their desks. Finally he finds out they are members of a secret society where membership offers many privileges. Wouldn't that be a dream come true if you could join a club like that? Well I don't know of any organization like that, but there is a growing group that gets to invest while avoiding many of the fees most investors pay — by using DRIPs and SPPs.

What are these? DRIPs stand for "dividend reinvestment plans" and SPPs are "stock purchase plans". Remember dividends are the cash companies send shareholders on a regular basis. You can either reinvest those dividends or spend them. DRIPs are the reinvestment option. This is important so I'll explain this concept using a simple story (from the Brothers Grimm)

> *A long time ago there was a shoemaker who had nothing except a single piece of leather. He left the leather out and went to bed. In the morning when he went downstairs, he found a perfect pair of shoes. A customer came into the store and quickly bought the shoes. The shoemaker used the money he had earned from the shoe sale to buy more leather to make two more pairs of shoes. In the morning he awoke to find two perfect pair of shoes — which again sold quickly. This went on for weeks, with the shoemaker continually reinvesting the money he'd earned from selling shoes into buying more leather to make even more shoes...*

When you register for a DRIP, your dividends are automatically retained by the company and used to purchase more shares. We'll go over how to get the whole process started a little later, but let's take a quick look at the effect of this strategy.

One of the most powerful outcomes from investing is the compounding effect over long periods of time. This factor is so powerful that Einstein said compound interest was the greatest mathematical discovery of all time! DRIPs add further power to the compounding effect — boosting your returns.

I'll create a quick example to demonstrate this strategy. Suppose there are twin 20-year-old brothers who buy 100 shares of a company called Consistent Corp and the shares cost $50 each (so a $5,000 total investment). Let's assume the company returns 12%/year to shareholders over the long-term — 8% by way of capital appreciation (increase in share price) and 4% from dividends.

The first brother keeps his shares (which is a good move). He collects the dividend every three months and spends it, but he never sells any of his shares. At 65, he's ready to retire and checks the value of his shares. His original $5,000 investment has grown to about **$160,000**. Not bad for a $5,000 investment, but nothing to write home about.

The second brother enrolled in the DRIP and systematically reinvested all his dividends (which is a great move). He kept his shares and continued to purchase more shares with his regular dividends being reinvested. At 65, his investment is worth about **$820,000**. With dividend reinvestment he has more than *5 times as much money as his brother*!

Now go back and look at the beginning of the example again. The return was a 12% total (8% capital and *only* 4% dividends). How is it that the total amount of money at retirement becomes five times greater when dividends are reinvested? These dividends represent only one third of the percentage rate of return. Isn't it interesting to note the importance of this reinvestment factor? Remember:

Dividends matter — a LOT! Reinvesting dividends will have a HUGE impact on how much wealth you can accumulate over time!

Just to quickly show the advantage of starting early, if someone had bought shares for these twins earlier, let's look at the impact. Suppose the father had bought 100 shares of the same company for these twins 10 years earlier and the investment is enrolled in the DRIP. At 65, the shares are worth over two million dollars. In fact, they are worth roughly **$2,550,000**! By starting a few years earlier, the final amount is much larger. This is why I decided to write the second section about investing for children within this book. They are "time millionaires" and with investing — time is a great asset! So remember:

Time is a huge factor with investing. Just as Archimedes said, "Give me a lever long enough and a fulcrum on which to place it and I shall move the world." Time is like a financial lever — even by starting with small amounts, time can create a huge amount of wealth!

This is why I'm a huge believer in implementing a DRIP strategy ASAP. If you also decide to initiate this plan for your children, you'll set them up for financial security. The compounding effect can be huge as they have time on their side.

The other benefit is that the whole DRIP concept is mechanical in nature — dividends get reinvested automatically at regular intervals. I'm going to expand on the fact

I mentioned earlier. *Investing properly is 90% emotional and only 10% intellectual.* Getting control of your emotions is a huge factor in success. To have faith in the companies you own after you've researched them and to keep them and not panic when the doomsayers and naysayers come out and explain why the world is coming to an end — that's the key to building (and keeping) wealth. This bears repeating:

> *Controlling your emotions is the key to successful stock invest-ing. There are always "clouds" on the horizon.*

When you make this strategy mechanical, it removes the emotional component which can cloud your decisions. You invest regularly whether the market is doing well or not. You begin to appreciate and accept stock market crashes a whole lot more — and don't lose sleep when the storm clouds gather. When the price of company shares fall, you can buy more through the automatic dividend reinvestments. This strategy followed over long period of time can create the proper attitude for investing and teach investors to focus on the dividend stream rather than being held captive to the ups and downs of the stock market.

> *The volatility of the stock market is just "noise" in the grand scheme of things. Ignore it — or better yet, use it to your advantage!*

If you follow the financial news, you'll quickly realize that the main focus in daily reports is on "how the market did today." During market sell-offs, you can see footage of traders in a panic — screaming orders at each other. Tensions increase, blood vessels pop with everyone scrambling to sell in a huge lemming-like stampede. These actions are not intellectual — they are emotional! In the long-run, these market panics don't amount to a hill of beans. The key is to not get all worked up over them. Better still; *don't* pay attention to business news. Ignore these panics — don't become imprisoned by them, but do benefit from them.

I'll use the example from Judo (a Japanese martial art) as a way of explaining this concept. As explained in *"Kodokan, What is Judo"*, "Victory over the opponent is achieved by giving way to the strength of the opponent, adapting to it and taking advantage of it, turning it, in the end, to your advantage."

Essentially in the world of investing, the sheer force of millions of investors with their control of billions of dollars is a force that you cannot overcome — you can't fight it. Like a small boat in a huge storm, you simply have to let the market go where the forces are pushing it. But you can use this volatility to your advantage. By using DRIPs and investing mechanically *without any thinking or emotions* — you actually benefit when markets crash — taking one of the perceived weaknesses of investing and turning it into a strength for your own accumulation of wealth and eventual financial freedom!

Here's how it all will work. When you're mechanically investing with DRIPs, you benefit from "dollar-cost averaging" which will actually outperform most investors. Here's an example to explain this concept.

Suppose $200 is invested *every month* in a recession-proof, stable, dividend-paying stock. This investment plan removes any thought or emotion and is followed mechanically regardless of the outlook of the market commentators. The stock market becomes volatile over a few months and here's what happens:

MONTH	INVESTMENT	STOCK PRICE	SHARES PURCHASED
1	$200	$50	4
2	$200	$100	2
3	$200	$20	10
4	$200	$50	4
Totals	**$800**		**20**

Let's take a quick look at this. The stock started the period at $50/share and also ended the period at $50/share (the same price). During the first month, you were able to buy 4 shares ($200 / $50 per share). Then the market outlook improved. In the second month, the investment sun was shining and people were happy. It was blue skies as far as the eye could see. The stock went up to $100 — which had investors popping the champagne corks and dancing in the streets. In that month, your regular $200 investment bought 2 shares ($200 / $100 per share).

Then the picture darkened. Any investor with two functioning brain cells could see the storm clouds gathering on the horizon — and they headed for cover! As everyone rushed to the exit doors at the same time, panic ensued. With whatever information was available during this time, the only logical conclusion was to sell — at any cost — and get to safety! During this month, your mechanical strategy went on doing what it always did — invest $200. This was the "dumb" strategy of simply ignoring all the information the other "sophisticated" investors had — and blindly investing. The old adage of, *"Ignorance is bliss"* applied to you in this case — you were ignorant of all the gloom that had gripped the market — and you were blissful in your bubble of oblivion. So this month your regular $200 bought 10 shares ($200 / $20 per share).

Finally, things returned to normal. Some of the storm clouds dissipated. The sun came out and a sense of relative calm ensued. The prudent "professional" investors now decided that buying shares in this company would be a good move and as the buyers returned, the price rose somewhat — returning to the original $50/share. Your regular investment strategy buys four shares this month ($200 / $50).

You didn't do any analysis or focus on media reports. You spent your time living your life — blissfully unaware of the turbulence. The result is that you bought more shares when the price was low and fewer when the price was high. In total you spent $800 and received 20 shares, so your cost per share is $800/20 = $40/share. The average price you paid is lower than the average stock price in 3 of the 4 months. Even though the beginning and ending price was $50.share, you bought your shares at a 20% discount to this. The $800 you invested is now worth (20 shares X $50/share) = $1,000. Because of the turbulence, you've gained 25% over this shore period of time — and you didn't have any of the worry the other investors had.

Now the above example is a little unrealistic in how much the imaginary stock fluctuated, but it's useful for explaining the premise of "dollar-cost averaging". This strategy by its very nature ensures that you buy more shares when the price is low and fewer shares when the price is high. There's no thinking or emotion involved — no sleepless nights or analysis required on your part. Simply ignore the noise and keep mechanically doing the same thing over and over for a long period of time — and outperform the vast majority of investors!

This in essence is how a DRIP would work. Every quarter, instead of the company sending you your regular dividend cheque, the money *automatically* gets reinvested in more shares at the prevailing stock price. Once it's set up, the whole thing is automatic!

It's the same with SPPs. Remember, SPPs stand for "Stock Purchase Plans", and this is how they work. A handful of companies in Canada offer SPPs along with their DRIPs and these entitle the owner to send cash at certain times of the year in order to purchases additional shares. The advantage of this is that there are no commission fees. You simply write a cheque and mail it. Your payment will be used to buy more shares. You can do this sporadically or at regular intervals. You can build up a sizeable position over time — even if you start with just one share. And the best part is that you can set this up without incurring any fees. You can start the whole process with less than $50 in some cases — so it's accessible to almost everyone.

Aside from these advantages, there are a few others I should mention at this point. One thing you must realize is that many "investors" are not investors at all — they are speculators. They watch the market daily and buy and sell as often as they brush their teeth. This impulse is encouraged by a daily diet of short-term forecasts that implore everyone to buy or sell certain stocks based on various short-term factors.

Let me clarify — I don't advocate buying and selling often. The most successful investors simply buy great companies and hold onto them — sometimes for decades. I follow this approach as I sell stocks about as often as February 29th rolls around — and only if there's a compelling reason to do so. This approach forces you to take a long time researching stocks to make sure you have the ones best suited for you. However, to make things easier I'm going to offer you an actual list of some possible stocks that offer DRIPs and SPPs that you can add to your portfolio a little later in the book.

DRIPs are perfect for instilling patience and calm in investors. When prices drop, you can see from your regular statement how this has helped you buy more shares. Your regular SPP payments also buy more shares — so you begin to look at stocks the same way you look at gasoline prices — you're encouraged to buy more when prices fall. In addition, selling is not as easy as simply calling your broker and screaming "sell" into the phone in a fit of panic. Selling the shares is more difficult using the DRIP approach (which we'll get into later) — and this adds another layer of protection against temporary irrational emotions.

This combination of factors — not needing a huge amount to get started, no fees, no research required once you get started, and regular statements that show you how market drops are helping you accumulate more shares creates a very powerful method for you to build wealth gradually over time without having to commit a lot of time reviewing your investments.

What stocks should you buy? How should you add to your investments over time? How should you construct your portfolio? The answers to these questions are the focus of the next chapter.

6

ONLY IN CANADA, *EH?*

*"The grass is always greener
(on the other side of the fence)"*

■ **Common Idiom**

When I first publicly revealed my investment strategy, there were many people who claimed that it was not the correct strategy. I questioned the wisdom of always "maximizing one's RRSP" and many people took exception to that. I rejected the "nest egg" approach in investing and instead focused on the "cash flow" approach. I shunned bonds in favour of blue-chip dividend-paying stocks. I ignored the idea of extensive diversification and focused on simple to understand, recession-proof businesses that had a history of raising their dividends over time. Many people disagreed with a lot of these ideas.

Ben Graham (the father of fundamental analysis) mentioned that investing is not a popularity contest. You are right or wrong *not* based on how many people agree with you, but whether or not you are correct in your analysis.

The information contained in the next few chapters will not parallel a lot of the information sold to the general public through advertising. It contradicts a lot of the conventional "wisdom" on investing. However, it offers a solid foundation on which to build a strong portfolio.

In order to keep things simple and to avoid as much tax and fees as possible, you should start your investment program using only Canadian stocks. DRIPs work well here and the dividends are not taxed excessively (or not at all in many cases). When you receive Canadian dividends, you have to "gross up" (tax jargon) the amount you received, but then there's an offsetting dividend tax credit. The calculation is rather complex, but I did go over it briefly in my first book, *STOP WORKING: Here's How You Can!* The important point to remember is that dividends from Canadian companies are very favourably taxed — so it's a great place to start on your journey to financial freedom. With foreign holdings, you pay a withholding tax (15% for US companies) right off the top. This amount can cut into the compounding effect and slow your wealth accumulation.

I know the standard dogma is that "Canada represents only 3% of the world economy, so by investing only in Canada you're missing out on 97% of the opportunities..." I feel this advice is somewhat self-serving as it leads investors to seek certain mutual funds so they can benefit from the various opportunities around the globe that they have no hope of investing in on their own. How about changing the above quote to, "Canada represents only 3% of the world economy, so by investing only in Canada you're missing out on 97% of the RISK..."

I'll examine a few facts. When you want to learn something, your first step should be to find people who have done what you want to do and perhaps emulate some of the factors that created success for them. My investing strategy was a combination of Warren Buffett (billionaire investor) and Peter Lynch (former star money manager and financial author) combined with some of my own ideas. When I first decided to write about investing, I didn't know exactly what the process would entail. I contacted a fellow named Alan Dickson who had written a couple of financial books and he helped me immensely. I also called David Chilton (author of *The Wealthy Barber* — the best-selling Canadian book ever) for some pointers. In fact, this book started my journey to financial freedom at such a young age and David was even more helpful in guiding me through the writing and publishing maze. By contacting people who had already done what I wanted to do, I was able to gain valuable information and this helped me reach my goals.

If we want to see how to make money, wouldn't it make sense to seek out how others have done it? As already mentioned, Forbes publishes a list of the world's richest people every year. Even though I have no dreams of being a billionaire, it's an interesting place to start. Simply put, I'd rather look at what wealthy people have done than seek advice from people who want to sell me investment products.

When I look down the Forbes list, I see people who have most of their net worth in the company they own.

They're not overly concerned with diversification — they're wealth is much more concentrated.

Let's look at an example. Do you know which fortune is the biggest on the list? Many people know that Bill Gates is the world's richest man, but he's not the holder of the biggest fortune. His mere $50 billion is dwarfed by the nearly $80 billion fortune of the Walton family (of Wal-Mart). The late founder Sam Walton would be the world's richest person if he were alive today. Instead, his five heirs each have a mere $16 billion. Most of that wealth is tied up in Wal-Mart.

Let's take a quick look at this retail juggernaut. How big is it? It employs over 1.4 million people. It represents 2% of US GDP (total amount of goods and services produced in an economy). Its revenues amount to over $280 billion US annually (and growing). If it were a country, it would be the 19th largest economy in the world. It's interesting to note that in spite of the impressive numbers listed above, Wal-Mart represents a mere 7% of the total retail market share in the US.

So the richest family fortune is invested primarily in the entity above — one company. How about investing exclusively in Canada? Here are some interesting facts.

Canada has a GDP of around $1.165 trillion (according to the CIA Fact Book), making it the 12th largest economy in the world. It's interesting to note that all 11 countries that place higher in total GDP have MUCH larger populations. Canada ranks 7th in GDP per person — so its citizens enjoy one of the highest standards of living on the planet. We possess a highly skilled workforce and advanced infrastructure. The rule of law is well entrenched and corruption is quite low by international standards. We've been endowed with tremendous resources — unparalleled in most countries. We are an emerging energy superpower with stated oil reserves second only to Saudi Arabia. Our fiscal situation with regards to government debt is gradually improving and we are an open economy with free trade with the largest economy in the world. Our predominant language — English — is the most important language in the world and our other official language — French, is also used in many countries. With immigrant communities we've created a lot of informal networks which can enhance trade and commerce.

Although Canada has some problems, it's a great place to invest due to its overall stability. Below is a list of Canadian Companies (and their ticker symbols) that offer DRIPs *and* SPPs. Many Canadian companies offer DRIPs, but only these few companies also offer SPPs. The advantage of having a DRIP combined with an SPP is that you can start very small and gradually add to your positions. This list is available in the *Canadian Moneysaver (www.canadianmoneysaver.ca)* magazine which also offers additional information about investing in general.

1. Pulse Data Inc (PSD)
2. Canadian General Investments (CGI)
3. BCE Inc (BCE)

4. Emera (EMA)

5. Transalta Corporation (TA)

6. Bank of Montreal (BMO)

7. TransCanada Corp (TRP)

8. National Bank (NA)

9. Bank of Nova Scotia (BNS)

10. Enbridge (ENB)

11. Fortis (FTS)

12. Canadian Imperial Bank of Commerce (CM)

13. TELUS (T.A)

14. Sun Life Financial (SLF)

15. Manulife (MFC)

16. Imperial Oil (IMO)

17. IPSCO (IPS)

18. Suncor Energy (SU)

19. Agnico Eagle Mines (AEM)

With the majority of companies listed above, you can buy as little as one share and then enrol in the DRIP and gradually add to your position through the SPP (with a few exceptions). Three or four holdings would be a great start to an investment portfolio. My approach focuses on simple to understand businesses that I am confident in. From the list above, I'll provide four examples of companies you could start with. This does not mean that the others are not suitable, it simply means that the businesses I will choose will be ones that I feel I know well enough to be willing to hold for a very long time. You can choose companies from this list to create your own DRIP portfolio or simply invest in the ones I've chosen.

1. Scotiabank

The truth is that in Canada, you can't go wrong by being an owner of any of the major banks. Over time they just make more money — even as we gripe about high fees. When Willie Sutton the bank robber was asked why he robbed banks, he replied "Because that's where the money is." The same can be said for bank investors. The reality is that the banks are great money-makers. I know that "historical results are no guarantee of future returns", but it's still interesting to look at this group. I was recently looking through the publication, *Money Reporter* when I came across the historical dividend history of the banks. They all have a great long-term history of paying *uninterrupted* dividends — Royal Bank with 137 years, Bank of Montreal with 178 years, CICB with 139 years, TD with 150 years, and Scotiabank with 174 years. Even the comparatively small Laurentian Bank has managed 136 consecutive years — a pretty consistent record. A history of dividend increases for Scotiabank was provided on page 30.

The big banks offer traditional mortgage lending, but their earnings come from a much broader source now. Credit cards with high interest rates have mushroomed over the last number of years. Every transaction that involves a credit card has the issuer making money. Banks have also moved into wealth management as they offer mutual funds and both discount and full-service brokerage services. Selling insurance is the next area opening up. Global expansion is also occurring as some banks have moved into the US market. Scotiabank has perhaps the most international operations with 12 million customers in over 50 countries around the world. Simply put, Scotiabank is in the money business — which has been great for shareholders! If you participate in the SPP, there is a $100 minimum amount that must be invested.

> *Banks make money. Every year they mail out little paper entitled, "Notice of Fee **Changes**". Many customers instantly throw it out. Next time you receive one of these notices, review it. It should be entitled, "Notice of Fee **Increases**". These increases are not good for customers, but great for shareholders!*

2. Enbridge Inc.

This is one of the companies I decided to invest some of my children's money in for a variety of reasons. The core business is pipelines and people need the oil and gas these pipelines transport in good times and bad. Once the pipelines are built, they continue to generate revenue year-in, year-out for a VERY long time. That's not all — Enbridge also owns Canada's largest natural gas distribution company with operations in Ontario, Quebec, and New York State. Over fifty years of dividend payments and above average returns seem to indicate this is a solid choice for any would-be investor. Unlike Scotiabank, there is no minimum amount that must be invested through the SPP. Here's a quick look at the dividend history from 1996–2006:

YEAR	DIVIDEND PER SHARE
1996	$0.53
1997	$0.56
1998	$0.60
1999	$0.64
2000	$0.70
2001	$0.76
2002	$0.83
2003	$0.92
2004	$1.04
2005	$1.15
2006	$1.23

Try turning your furnace off next January. How long before you turn it back on? Every time you hear your furnace turn on — Enbridge is making money — and using that money to raise their dividend!

3. Fortis

This company is unique in a number of respects. First, it owns a number of regulated utilities in Canada, as well as in Belize, the Cayman Islands, and the Turks and Caicos Islands — an unconventional mix. It also combines these holdings with 18 hotels and 2.7 million square feet of commercial real estate in 7 different provinces in Canada. In addition, while many head offices of Canadian companies are located in Toronto or Calgary, Fortis is based out of St. Johns, Newfoundland. I'm usually not a huge fan of companies that are not focused on a core competency (one specialized business), but results speak for themselves. Fortis has a good track record of increasing dividends over time with dividend raises every year since 1974. A dividend of around 8 cents in 1972 has grown to 64 cents at the time of this writing. Here's a ten-year summary:

YEAR	DIVIDEND PER SHARE
1997	$0.44
1998	$0.45
1999	$0.45
2000	$0.46
2001	$0.47
2002	$0.49
2003	$0.52
2004	$0.54
2005	$0.59
2006	$0.67

At first glance, the dividend growth rate of Fortis does not seem very impressive. Here I would like to introduce to you another important concept when considering dividends — "payout ratio". The payout ratio is simply the percentage of every dollar earned in profits that is paid out in dividends. So if your company earns $1 in profits and pays 40 cents out as dividends (and keeps 60 cents to reinvest in growth), the payout ratio would be 40%.

In the case of Fortis, in 1998 the company had a payout ratio of 85% (85 cents of every $1 in profit was paid out in dividends, with only 15% being reinvested). In 2006, the payout ratio had dropped to 46%. So in 2006, over 50% of the profits were being reinvested in the company. As you reinvest more money into buying assets that produce more income, you usually see more income growth. As income grows faster, dividends usually grow faster. This is what I would expect to happen with Fortis in the future.

Once you are a shareholder, you can add money through the SPP in amounts as little as $100.

Fortis is the same as Enbridge, except it deals with electricity. How long could you live without power?

4. Imperial Oil

If you drive a car, chances are that at some point in time you've used gas from Imperial Oil. Started in 1880, Imperial Oil is one of the largest producers of crude oil in Canada and the country's biggest refiner and marketer of petroleum products. A quick look at their website shows dividend payments going back to 1947 with numerous dividend increases. Simply put, I like oil as an investment. It's an indispensable commodity required for our modern world. Money, from a historical perspective, usually gravitates towards those with oil. Rockefeller was super-rich because of oil. Sheiks in the Middle East live lavish lifestyles simply because the patch of desert where they live covers a virtual sea of oil. The richest and only debt-free province in Canada is Alberta and this is due to oil. The only potential concern is that Exxon Mobil Corp. owns 69.6% of Imperial Oil and some day may wish to own the whole company. Should this occur, you might end up suddenly learning that your shares have been bought out. Overall, there are worse things that could happen. There is a $50 minimum required investment to add shares through the SPP. You can get the dividend history going back to 1947 by going to the website *www.imperialoil.ca.* Click on "Information for Investors", then on the list on the left-hand side of your screen scroll down to "Your Imperial Oil Shares". Once you've clicked on that, scroll down to "Historical share prices and dividends" and click. There has been a great history of paying increasing dividends. Here's a quick ten-year summary:

YEAR	DIVIDEND PER SHARE
1996	$0.68
1997	$0.73
1998	$0.74
1999	$0.75
2000	$0.78
2001	$0.83

2002	$0.84
2003	$0.87
2004	$0.88
2005	$0.94
2006	$0.96

Note Imperial Oil had a 3 for 1 stock split in 2006. Currently Imperial Oil has a payout ratio of around 10%, which means almost 90% of its profits are being reinvested for growth! I would expect stronger dividend growth in the future.

Oil is the foundation of our modern society. Every product in existence was produced and shipped using oil. Without oil, our modern society would cease to exist.

With these four holdings you can get started with DRIPs. These companies are large and an integral part of the Canadian economy with long histories of increased earnings and dividends. Even though this example portfolio only represents four holdings, you have exposure to a wide range of businesses located in a number of countries. You can also look at the list above and see if there are any of the other companies that appeal to you. One note — two insurers (Manulife and Sun Life) charge fees for their plans, so you would have to have a compelling reason to invest in these companies in order to compensate for this drawback.

The four companies listed above offer a great start on your road to financial freedom. The next chapter will offer an additional suggestion to broaden your portfolio.

7

MORE *TRUST* IN CANADA

*"Well, real estate is always good,
as far as I'm concerned"*

▓ **Donald Trump**

There is a way to broaden your portfolio after you have the first phase of good Canadian stocks underway. You can add this diversification by adding income trusts.

Income trusts are business entities that are taxed differently than corporations. The last decade or so has seen an explosion in the number of income trusts offered. Personally, income trusts play a huge part in my portfolio as they pay out most of their earnings in distributions (trusts' version of dividends).

Changes to the tax laws have called into question how profitable trusts will be going forward. On October 31, 2006, the finance minister announced a new policy of taxing trusts starting in 2011. It was interesting to see the reaction of many investors to this announcement and it reminded me of an old story.

A long time ago, two shoe salesmen decide to head out into the great unknown to seek their fortune. Finally they arrived at their destination which was inhabited by primitive tribes. The first shoe salesman takes a quick look around and quickly heads back to his home office. He reports to his supervisor that the whole trip was a complete waste of time. He exclaims, "Nobody there even wears shoes, they all run around barefoot!"

The second salesman is not heard from for a very long time. Finally, he returns and reports back to the same supervisor about his stunning success. He explains, "It was great! I found a huge market where nobody even owned shoes — the poor people were all running around barefoot! I also had the whole market to myself as there were no other shoe salesmen in the entire area!"

A similar situation occurred after the income trust announcement — which caused the prices of many trusts to plummet. I heard radio talk shows where callers were lamenting about how "billions of dollars in wealth had virtually disappeared overnight!" The whole trust market was now doomed and people relying on these investments were now destined for poverty. But the whole kafuffle created a great opportunity and I used this correction to buy some units. Going forward, regardless of what happens, I still think these business entities will continue to operate, make money, and continue to write cheques to their shareholders.

Here is a copy of an article I wrote for *Canadian Moneysaver* magazine in early November 2006. This was right after the big announcement about the taxation of trusts. The article is useful in answering two questions I'm often asked:

1. Are income trusts still okay to invest in?
2. What situation causes stocks to go "on sale"?

This article was written for those who are sophisticated investors. If you are not one of these people, feel free to skip the article — as it is not essential to the beginner strategy outlined in this book.

On October 31, income trust investors got a trick instead of a treat from the federal government. In spite of a promise not to tax income trusts, a new taxation plan was announced. The next day, many trusts' market prices plummeted between 15–20%.

I retired at 34 by buying steady dividend-paying blue-chip stocks with a very healthy dose of high yielding income trusts. This surprise announcement wiped over $30,000 off my portfolio in a single day. However, with my strategy, I don't focus on my portfolio value as I know it will go up and down like a yo-yo. I focus on the cash being paid to me on a regular basis — this is the income I need to fund my very early retirement.

With the announcement, the ability of trusts to pay their generous distributions has been reduced. Starting in 2011 (existing trusts have a four-year grace period); they will pay taxes, which will reduce the cash they have available to send to unit holders. The tax rate at that time will be 31.5% (from what I've read), so almost a third less cash will be available.

How did I react to all this? With lightening speed, I leapt to action and did...absolutely nothing. There was no chance for anyone to sell before the plunge. The underlying fundamentals of the income trust model had changed, but these changes had already affected market prices. There was no point in selling. I called my MP, the PMO, and Jim Flaherty's office, and my opinions were duly recorded, but I'm not holding my breath waiting for action. The rest of the day was spent taste-testing my kids Halloween treats to make sure they were "totally safe for their consumption" — as I explained it to them.

Then what? The next step was to examine the universe of trusts to see if I could perhaps find some oversold gems available through all this. So I went to the Dominion Bond Rating Service website (www.dbrs.com) and clicked on "Income Funds". I recorded all the names of trusts that had a stability rating of STA-1 or STA-2 (the lower the number, the more stable the distributions are according to DBRS). I found some familiar names — many trusts I own and mention in my book, "STOP WORKING: Here's How You Can!" But some prices still seemed very pricey. For example, Pembina Pipelines had fallen from almost $18/unit to around $13/unit (a pretty sizeable retreat). But I had bought it for $7.75 during the Tech Bubble, so I was loathe paying almost twice that price for more units. So on I went until I fell into hot water, or more precisely water heaters.

For anyone who is familiar with the strategy I used to retire at 34, they'll see the appeal of this type of business right away. Simple, recession-proof business with no fancy technological breakthroughs coming that can confuse me (which isn't too hard on most days). Regardless of the season, economy, fashion trends, whatever, people will use hot water. I had a 15-year-old tank burst a few years ago, and just called the company and they replaced it right away. Simple. I examined Consumers' Waterheater Income Fund a little closer. The cost of a water heater is about 40 cents a day, so it's not a huge expense for consumers. The number of water heater rentals has increased over the last 16 years at a rate of 4%/year, and they service areas of growing population mostly in southern Ontario so the number of customers should keep growing. They should also be able to raise rental prices by the rate of inflation over time.

Over the last few years, the distributions were $1.05 in 2003, $1.067 in 2004, $1.12 in 2005, and $1.19 projected in 2006. Next year, if monthly distributions remain constant, distributions will be $1.23. So there's been slow but steady growth. Meanwhile, the unit price fell from around $16 to around $12 after the announcement. I bought some units on November 3 at $12.65.

Any time one buys stocks or income trusts, there are always risks. On many occasions I've single-handedly proven the second part of Einstein's assertion when he said, "The only two infinite things are the universe and human stupidity". I'm not a professional stock picker or analyst, but here was my thinking on this....

With $1.23 in distributions and a unit price of $12.65, my immediate yield will be 9.7% taxed like interest income. If I assume prices rise 2%/year, and volume also rises at

2%/year (half the historical rate of growth), then I can assume the trust will earn roughly 4% more each year for the next 4 years. If they also raise the distribution by that amount, then the payout will grow from $1.23 now, to $1.44 by 2011 (when the announced taxes kick in). Then tax will be 31.5% (from what I read), so a 31.5% reduction is (1.44 x .685 = 99 cents). With approximately a 99 cent annual distribution in 2011, the yield on my purchase price will be 7.8%. Now since the government wants to "level the playing field between income trusts and corporations", I would expect this new reduced distribution to receive favourable tax treatment like dividends currently do (with the dividend tax credit).

So with this investment, I expect to receive a regularly taxed 9.8% yield which should rise to 11.5% by 2011 (when the new taxes kick in). Then I will get a tax-advantaged 7.8% yield which should rise slightly faster than the rate of inflation. The unit price should also be supported at this lower level as the new taxation rules have already been announced. With the first of the baby boomers hitting 60 this year, I feel the demand for yield will not disappear as people will shift money from more speculative stocks into stable cash generators that are boring but stable.

So although I am not happy at all about the government's announcement, I'm hoping to find a silver lining. I made my decision with imperfect information and I could be proven wrong, but that's the nature of investing — low risk is never no risk.

Since I purchased this trust, unit prices have risen to over \$17/unit — or almost 40% in six months — but that fact is totally unimportant. The real story is that a few months after I bought the units, they raised their distribution by 4.9% (a little more than the 4% I had assumed in my analysis) to \$1.29/year. Since I had bought the units at \$12.65 each, they were now giving me over 10% every year on my initial investment.

This was an actual purchase I made and it shows the analysis I went through. However, the thrust of the strategy outlined in this book is buying great companies without having to do any research on price — so we need an investment that offers DRIPs and SPPs. It's interesting to note that there are more trusts that offer DRIPs and SPPs in Canada than stocks. However, there are a few reasons why I wouldn't load up on these. First, a lot of the trusts that offer DRIPs and SPPs are energy trusts. These trusts own oil and gas assets and simply pump it out of the ground and sell it. Historically, they've been able to pay out high distributions and keep replenishing their reserves by buying oil and gas properties from exploration companies. I'm not comfortable with having an asset that is going to deplete over time without replenishment, so I would not add new money to these through a DRIP. In the case of my children, the cash being spun off from an energy trust they own is being reinvested into another company.

Second, a lot of these trusts have a minimum investment of \$500 or \$1000. That may be a reasonable entry point for some people, but with the idea of starting very small and adding slowly, I think these amounts are too large.

I'm not going to list all the trusts that offer DRIPs and SPPs here. For a detailed list of all Canadian securities (stocks and trusts) that offer DRIPs, simply go to *www.cdndrips.blogspot.com*. Remember when you are looking at starting out, you should focus on companies that have SPPs as well as DRIPs — which is indicated here. This list will also show you which companies offer discounts on additional purchases made through their DRIP plans. These discounts can also help you on your road to financial freedom, but remember that the most important criteria to follow is to only invest in quality companies that have a bright future. A discount won't help you if you are buying low-quality securities.

I have selected one holding that I feel is of good quality. I actually own this in my own portfolio. The price has risen a lot since I originally purchased it, but with DRIPs you can add to your position slowly and take advantage of any market corrections automatically.

1. Riocan

Riocan is a REIT which stands for Real Estate Investment Trust. It is the largest REIT exclusively focused on retail real estate. It owns a lot of the big box power centres that have numerous tenants like Wal-Mart, Shoppers Drug Mart, Canadian Tire, Zellers, to name a few. These supermarket anchored shopping centres are essential for people who do their regular shopping there. Once one of these centres has been built in your neighbourhood, they have a captive market as people will not drive more than they have to while running their errands.

Could you live your life without ever shopping at stores? A lot of these stores are owned by REITs, which collect the rent and send it to their shareholders.

Once again, after you own a single unit, you can participate in the DRIP and SPP. Every dividend will be reinvested in additional units. One bonus you get with Riocan is that with each dividend reinvested, you purchase more shares at a 3.1% discount automatically by simply being enrolled in the DRIP! I love free money — and that's exactly what this amounts to! This is one of those discounts mentioned above. With the SPP you can buy additional units without incurring any fees. The minimum investment is $250 each time you want to buy more units.

Riocan's history has been pretty good. The distributions have risen consistently since the 1995 distribution of $1.15 per unit (with a 2for1 stock split in 1998). Remember, a stock split gives you more shares for each original share — in Riocan's case, there are now two shares for every original share owned in 1995. Here's a quick chart of the distribution history (rounded to the nearest penny):

YEAR	DISTRIBUTION PER UNIT
1995	$1.15
1996	$1.30
1997	$1.55
****	**2for1 Split**

1998	$0.95
1999	$1.04
2000	$1.07
2001	$1.08
2002	$1.11
2003	$1.14
2004	$1.23
2005	$1.27
2007	$1.30

**<u>Note</u> Because of the stock split, each distribution after 1997 must be multiplied by 2. So if you owned 1 share in 1995, your initial income of $1.15 per year has grown to ($1.30 X 2) = $2.60 per year by 2006.

This is pretty simple….think about it. If you were to ask someone who bought their house in 1970 how much they paid, they would give you a price that would be equivalent to the cost of an average car today. Real Estate prices rise over time — both houses and commercial real estate. As prices rise, rents also rise. Over time, Riocan collects the rent cheques and raises the rent every so often — and then sends the money to all its investors. The big bonus of investing in Riocan instead of real estate directly is that you have no hassles — they do it for you.

So as the old expression goes, *"Don't wait to buy land, buy land and wait"* — and collect the ever-increasing rent cheques!

The next section will look at a few other possible investments — in the US.

8

WHAT ABOUT AMERICAN DRIPS?

"The business of America is business."

▓ **Calvin Coolidge** (former US president)

Aside from the fact that most Canadians prefer certain aspects of our way of life to the American way, the reality is that the US is an economic giant within the world economy. The old saying, "When America sneezes, Canada catches a cold", is a truism that can't be denied. The US is the largest and most technologically advanced country in the world. It has been called, "The capital of capitalism". If you look at the world's most powerful brands which are assessed by those involved in Global Marketing, Microsoft topped the list. This was followed by GE and Coca-Cola to round out the top three. In fact, 8 of the top 10 brands in the world were American. The simple reality is that a large number of US companies have grown to dominate many areas of the world economy.

These companies have the opportunity to grow and offer their products to more consumers every year. With the emerging middle class in both China and India well underway, these companies stand to profit and grow for decades to come.

There are other important factors. Even though there is a withholding tax on US dividends of 15%, there are certain advantages to investing south of the 49th parallel. With so many really great global companies your opportunities are almost limitless. Once you've started with some of the great Canadian companies mentioned in the last chapter, you have the option of adding more diversity and industries by adding some US holdings.

How can you ascertain which companies to invest in and what should you look for?

As mentioned, the reason for going south of the border (and it's *not essential* but can deepen your portfolio), is that there are some great companies with global reach there. You're looking for companies with long operating histories which will consistently raise their dividends over time. In the past I have mentioned that if you look for "High Dividend Achievers" (companies that have increased their dividends consecutively for 10 years or more) that you would be building a solid foundation. With DRIPs, I would ratchet up the criteria. I'm going to advocate only looking at the "Dividends Aristocrats" (Companies that have 25 or more years of increasing dividends). Out of the thousands of public companies in the US, less that 60 make this elite list of steady dividend payers. If you want to review this list, the easiest way to do it is to Google "Dividend Aristocrats". This list is a great starting point. From here you can find companies you understand that also have a good DRIP program.

The point I'd like to reiterate here is that expanding to the US in not necessary. With the few investments I've mentioned in the previous two chapters, you can build up a pretty diversified, quality portfolio that should serve you well over time. I prefer to keep things simple and I would start with these five investments previously mentioned. This chapter is for people who absolutely want to include US investments in their DRIP plan. For those who don't feel the need to do this, you can skip to the next chapter.

Once again, the first thing you must remember about adding US DRIPs to your plan is that you will have to pay a 15% withholding tax on any dividends you receive and that this tax is *not* paid on Canadian holdings. This 15% can have a huge effect over time. The second factor that can reduce the appeal of US holdings is that you are holding investments in a foreign currency. The US dollar has been the world's reserve currency for a long time. It's accepted in more places than any other currency, but recently it has hit a bit of a rough patch. The US has gone from being the world's biggest creditor nation (lending money to the world), to being the world's biggest debtor nation (borrowing money from the world). It constantly has a huge trade deficit (buys more from the world than it sells) and its government constantly runs deficits in the hundreds of billions of dollars every year. This is in contrast to the Canadian situation whereby we have a massive trade surplus and have had government surpluses for a decade. In that time, while American debt has soared, we've actually repaid part of our debt. This repayment of debt has the effect of strengthening our currency.

I'm not an economist, but from the information above, moving money from Canadian investments to US investments may present some problems if the US dollar keeps falling. However, if you buy US investments that derive the majority of their income internationally, then you'd be partially insulated from any drops in the US dollar. As these companies earn their money in foreign currencies, the effect of a dropping dollar is muted because a large part of their business is outside North America.

The final argument against DRIPping in the US (at least in the beginning) is the complexity it adds. There are obstacles to overcome in order to DRIP in the US. Robert Gibb has written a number of articles on this subject, and they can be found in previous editions of *Canadian Moneysaver* magazine or also online at *"The Drip Investing Resource Center"*. I found the following information from an article entitled, *"Dripping south into the US"* which I'll share with you.

The first hurdle you must clear if you want to DRIP in the US is that the US Securities and Exchange Commission requires that the purchase of US stocks or bonds must be made through a US bank or a branch of a foreign bank that is physically located in the US. Fortunately for Canadians, our banks have been expanding into the US over the last number of years, so you can find Canadian banks physically operating in the US.

US dollar accounts opened at your local bank branch won't work and any cheques you send will be rejected. For US DRIPs, you must open a US dollar account with cheques that are cashable at a branch of that bank in the US. This type of account will have US transfer codes at the bottom of the cheque.

Apparently some of these hurdles might have been removed or are in the process of being removed. The landscape is constantly changing, so for up-to-date information on US DRIPs (or any DRIP info), I would recommend going to *www.dripinvesting.org*. Once you've gone to this site, you can click on "Articles" and see if there is an article that has been written that answers your questions, or you can click on "Community" and choose the appropriate subject and ask your question to board participants. For many US stocks, you can go to the company's website and there is usually specific information about the company's DRIP or SPP (called OCPs in the US). Another good source of information is a book written by Charles Carlson entitled, *"Buying Stocks Without a Broker"*. Once again, it's best to recheck the information as the companies do change their DRIP policies from time to time.

In my personal portfolio, the majority of my holdings are in Canadian securities, but I do have a few US holdings to add a little more diversification. Below I'll give you a list of companies that I think would be great additions to your portfolio if you decide that you want to add some US companies through DRIPping. They are all "Dividend

Aristocrats" (companies that have increase earnings for 25 or more consecutive years).

In this list of potential candidates, I chose companies that don't charge fees to participate in their DRIPs and SPPs. Once again, SPPs are referred to as OCPs (optional cash purchases) in the US, but they operate the same way. You've probably heard of the companies I'll list below and you can easily check out other companies you're familiar with by going to their websites and seeing if they offer DRIPs and OCPs (and also if they charge any fees).

1. Johnson and Johnson

One of the great US companies that has a long history of profitable growth, JNJ has a no-fee drip and a cash purchase plan. This company is a model of stability. Started over 100 years ago in the 1880s, JNJ now operates in three main segments which include consumer products, pharmaceuticals, and medical devices. The company operates in over 175 countries around the world. I've owned this stock for a few years and have benefited from its rising dividend — something that has occurred every year for the past 45 years. In addition to its glorious past, JNJ is extremely well-positioned to benefit from the general population aging occurring in so many countries today. Simply put, as people age, they consume more health care related products — and JNJ is the most diversified company in this area.

Here's a quick look at its 10-year dividend payment history:

YEAR	DIVIDEND PER SHARE
1997	$0.43
1998	$0.49
1999	$0.55
2000	$0.62
2001	$0.70
2002	$0.80
2003	$0.93
2004	$1.10
2005	$1.28
2006	$1.46

The dividend from 1997–2006 climbed over 300%. This is a solid dividend payer that should keep cranking out huge amounts of cash to shareholders.

Health care products are purchased regardless of the state of the economy. As people age, they spend more on health care — so companies that provide health care products make more money!

2. Pepsico

Pepsico offers a low-cost way to accumulate shares through its "Buydirect" plan. There is a $10 initial enrolment fee, but once paid, all optional cash investments and dividend reinvestments are free. Pepsi is known as the strong number 2 in the Cola wars, but it's much larger than that. A few years ago it was the largest fast food operator in the world (even bigger than McDonald's) with it's ownership of KFC, Pizza Hut, and Taco Bell. It spun those off, but since then purchased Quaker Oats (which owned Gatorade). So Pepsi is a huge operator in the soft drink market, a leader in the sports drink market with Gatorade, and owner of Tropicana. In addition to this, it is the largest snack food maker in North America with it's ownership in Frito-Lay. If you've ever eaten potato chips, chances are they were made by Pepsi. As many large countries emerge economically and create a large middle class, more and more people will be consuming these products. Here's how feeding the cravings for chips and pop have fed the hunger Pepsico shareholders have had for dividends over the last ten years:

YEAR	DIVIDENDS PER SHARE
1997	$0.49
1998	$0.51
1999	$0.53
2000	$0.56
2001	$0.58
2002	$0.60
2003	$0.63
2004	$0.85
2005	$1.01
2006	$1.16

Products that go in people's mouths have strong brand loyalty. People buy these products over and over — so the companies that own these brands keep making money.

3. 3M Company

3M offers a dividend reinvestment plan and accepts voluntary cash purchases of shares (without you having to pay any fees). 3M has paid dividends since 1916 and has 49 straight years of dividend increases. It operates in six different segments — industrial and transportation; healthcare; display and graphics; consumer and office; safety, security and protection services; and electro and communications — owing brands that range from Post-it notes to Scotch-Brite. With more than 69,000 employees selling products in nearly 200 countries and sales exceeding $22 billion dollars, this is a huge company with a very impressive long-term track record. Here's the brief ten-year summary of dividend payments:

YEAR	DIVIDENDS PER SHARE
1997	$1.06
1998	$1.10
1999	$1.12
2000	$1.16
2001	$1.20
2002	$1.24
2003	$1.32
2004	$1.44
2005	$1.68
2006	$1.84

It would be difficult to live in modern society without using any products that have been developed by 3M. This stock operates throughout the overall economy.

Simply put — five stocks can be adequate diversification when you're starting out, and you can easily choose
the five I listed in previous chapters and stay in Canada.
Warren Buffett held his portfolio of over $5 Billion US in
just five stocks back in 1989 — when $5 Billion was a lot
of money! However, if you want to increase the number of
holdings in your portfolio and add some US companies,
the three listed above are strong candidates with long
operating histories. If you want to find other potential candidates, stick with the *"Dividend Aristocrats"* I mentioned
earlier, and look at *Value Line* (available of major libraries)
to get additional information.

The next chapter is going to give you a basic step-by-
step guide for getting started in DRIPs and SPPs.

> ****Note** Terms and conditions of DRIP/SPP or OCP plans can
> change from time to time so check the company website or
> transfer agent before deciding to buy the shares. This will
> only take you a few minutes.

9

GETTING THE FIRST SHARE — A STEP-BY-STEP GUIDE

"The longest journey starts with a single step"

 Lao Tse

With the DRIP method of investing, buying the right kind of stock is important, but since you are investing small amounts of money over a long period of time, you simply don't have to worry about whether the stock is cheap enough to buy or not. All of your attention should be focused on the quality of the company — not its price. View these companies from a long-term perspective — they're like a marriage "death 'til us part" sort of arrangement. Dollar-cost averaging will work to your favour as you acquire more shares when the price is cheap and less shares when the price is expensive. You set the mechanical approach on autopilot and automatically accumulate wealth while focusing on living life.

So here is exactly how to get this whole process accomplished, in a simple step-by-step format. This is precisely what I would do if I was starting this strategy today. I have to give you a warning right from the beginning — this chapter is meant to guide you through a lot of legal and procedural issues you will face when you are getting your first share. As such, this chapter is somewhat dry and complex. However, it's essential to get your first share to embark on your journey to financial freedom. Just like anything new — learning it for the first time can be difficult and even daunting. Once you get started, it becomes easier. You might have to reread the chapter a few times or refer to it while you are completing the whole process. Once you've accomplished all this once, the next time should be easier. So here we go on a step-by-step journey:

1) Choose a company or companies you feel you want to invest in and make sure that they don't levy fees or other constraints for participating in their DRIP/SPP programs. You can check their website for details on their programs or call their investor relations department.

2) Focus on Canadian companies for simplicity (when you're starting out).

3) Don't invest in too many companies as this is unnecessary when you are starting small. Here is the list of initial candidates we covered earlier:

Scotiabank
Enbridge

Imperial Oil

Fortis

Riocan REIT

You can also look at the list available online at *www. cdndrips.blogspot.com* for other possible candidates. Remember, many companies in Canada offer DRIPs but not SPPs. The problem with this type of situation is that if you are starting with only one share and the company does not offer an SPP, then you are not going to add any shares over time as you won't be able to send in extra money for additional purchases. So you *need* companies that offer both DRIPs and SPPs to get started. So the list of five companies above is a great place to start.

With DRIPs and SPPs, the most difficult part is at the beginning — buying that elusive first share. After that, things can move along pretty smoothly. The easiest way to start your DRIP plan is to open a discount brokerage account. Remember that the reason you are using a DRIP and SPP strategy is so you can buy shares without incurring brokerage fees — so this is simply a temporary step to get you started. Every one of the big banks has their own discount brokerage. To set up your DRIP/SPP strategy using a brokerage account:

1) Visit any major bank branch and tell them you would like to open a discount brokerage account. You might have to call ahead to make an appointment.

The fees and commissions charged by the different brokerages are similar — so for simplicity we'll look at one of them as an example — TD Waterhouse. There you can open an account with no minimum balance as long as you sign up for "e-service" (as it's called). Basically you open a brokerage account at the bank and then as soon as they give you your password, you log onto their website and click on e-service. With this service, you will not receive regular paper statements from the broker — but you won't need them. Signing up for e-service allows you to avoid any inactivity fees (fees charged for not doing many transactions).

2) Once you have an account, it costs $29 to invest in 1 to 1,000 shares of any company. The cost for a share certificate (you need a certificate to get started) is $50, so the total cost for getting your first share is ($29 + $50) = $79 (plus the cost of the share)

3) These costs seem expensive, but once the DRIP plan is all set up, you should never pay any brokerage fees again.

Note First, you must buy your initial share, *then* contact the broker and request a share certificate (takes 1–2 weeks).

This essentially is the lazy way to get started with your first share. It requires no research once you've initiated the process as you can simply add extra money at regular intervals to purchase more shares of the companies you've chosen and the power of dollar-cost averaging will ensure you are always buying more shares when the price is low and fewer shares when the price is high.

Don't mention this DRIP strategy you've embarked on to your broker as they won't like losing the ability to charge you commissions every time you buy more shares. They will tell you about *their* DRIP plans. Here's some important info:

1) These brokerage "DRIPs" are known as "synthetic" DRIPs and you can only reinvest full shares, not fractional shares, so it would not work if you are starting with just one share.

2) If you want to invest in more shares over time, you have to pay a commission (usually $25–$30 depending of the broker) each time you add shares to your portfolio. With company SPPs that I've been detailing, once you've set it up there are usually no fees.

The DRIPs offered by brokers are NOT the same as DRIPs sponsored by the companies themselves.

By following the above steps, you have started on your journey to financial freedom. However, if you want to be *really* frugal, there is an even cheaper alternative to getting that first share. In fact the *cheapest* alternative is to go to a share exchange board. Here people will offer to sell you one of their shares or you can trade them for different shares you don't already have and you can do this *absolutely FREE!*

Here's how you would accomplish this:

1) Go to a Canadian share exchange board. You can find one at the DRiP Investing Resource Center. The exact website is *www.dripinvesting.org*.

2) When you get to the website, click on "Community" then click on "Share Exchange".

3) Type a message detailing which companies you are interested in investing in (you can look at the other messages for a guideline of how this is done). You might want to include an email address so you can discuss the details personally.

4) If you find someone willing to sell you a share (and you don't have any shares to trade at this point), you can pay a $10 courtesy "fee" plus the cost of the share to get the whole process completed.

The $10 courtesy "fee" is actually just to cover the cost of parking or other miscellaneous expenses the person doing you this favour might incur. Generally you send the person who is selling you the share a cheque for the price of the share plus the $10 "fee" and include a self-addressed envelope (The share price is usually the closing price on an agreed upon date and this figure is confirmed by email before you send the cheque). The person sending you the share will then deposit your cheque and send you the certificate for one share as soon as your cheque clears. *Make sure you send the exact name you want the share registered in — this is very important.*

Now, there is an issue of trust here. The person you send your cheque to might cash your cheque and never send you the share. When I brought this up with Robert Gibb, someone I would call a DRIP investing guru, he mentioned that with the few thousand transactions that had occurred through this site to date, this issue had never arisen. Robert is very active in the DRIP community and I would strongly urge you read whatever he has to say on the topic. He is a contributing editor for *Canadian Moneysaver* magazine where he's written numerous articles on DRIPs. A lot of the information for this chapter came from Robert.

Once these steps are completed you wait to receive your first share. When you do receive the share you will notice that the share is registered to the person who sent it to you (it has their name on the front), but on the back there is a section entitled, "Transfer of Ownership" and your name and information should appear there with a signature guarantee from a bank.

Getting the first share is simply a mechanism to become a shareholder. At this point it doesn't matter whether you used a broker or an exchange board to get to this stage. Your real aim here is to get into the company DRIP/SPP. So now that you've acquired that first share, here's what to do:

1) Go to the transfer agent's website.

There are basically two possible transfer agents — Computershare or CIBC Mellon. If you don't know who the transfer agent is, log onto the website of the company you just bought a share in and click on their investor relations icon. There should be some information about who the transfer agent is. If you can't find it, simply call the company's investor relations number and they'll be able to tell you.

2) On the transfer agent's website, click on the company you just purchased your share certificate for.

3) Download the DRIP/SPP forms (or have them mailed to you)

The first time you do this it might be confusing so I would advise you to click on the "contact us" icon and call the transfer agent (they are usually very helpful). Explain to them that you own a share of the company in question and want to enrol in the DRIP and SPP, so you need these forms. You need to do this to enrol in the DRIP *and* SPP — this is important. Also, ask the transfer agent what the minimum SPP amount is and also the correct mailing address.

Once you've filled out the forms, include these forms, the share certificate (if you acquired the share from the exchange board) and a cheque and mail it to the transfer agent. *Make sure the cheque is for an amount greater than the value of one share and also at least equal to the minimum SPP amount the transfer agent told you about.*

What usually happens at this stage is that the transfer agent will process your share and then send you an "anti-money laundering" form. They will not process your SPP and DRIP until you fill this form out. Simply fill the form out and send it back and they should process everything. After a while they will mail you a share certificate in your name. You will also receive a statement confirming you are in the DRIP plan and showing how many shares your cheque purchased through the SPP. Once you reach this stage, there are no more headaches (I know it was a long journey).

Now you can leisurely send in a cheque whenever you feel like it (you are under no obligation though). You can decide to make regular payments if you like (following the "pay yourself first" idea), but you have to check and see how often the company will accept SPP deposits (some are monthly, some are quarterly). Your dividends will automatically be reinvested forever — until you send them a letter telling them to stop.

I understand that all this information is overwhelming, but once you've completed the process, the whole thing chugs along automatically. The only effort on your part is sending in a cheque whenever *you* want. Also once you've completed the process once, the next time it's a piece of cake — sort of like riding a bike! You are now a member of the "DRIP/SPP "cult".

Now the DRIPpers are an interesting lot. They are loathe to pay unnecessary fees to banks or brokerages, so they help each other out. The idea is that once you're up and running and in the DRIP and SPP, it's time to *pay it forward*. In other words, you make that same share certificate available to another person so that they can enter the wonderful world of DRIPs. You also charge the $10 courtesy "fee", so in effect, the whole process has cost you nothing (except for the cost of a few stamps for mailing). You get your original $10 back. Since you are already enrolled in the plan and are a registered shareholder through the plan, you now don't need the 1 share in certificate form anymore.

Another option is trading the share. With your share certificate, you can trade it for a different share. For example, suppose you had Scotiabank and its stock price was $40, and you wanted a share in Enbridge and it was priced at $30. You could send your $40 Scotiabank share to another board member and they would send you one $30 Enbridge share and a $10 cheque. Again, this costs you essentially nothing.

Whether you sell the share or trade it, you are doing yourself and someone else a favour — it's *win-win*.

But what about the ins and outs of registering shares in somebody else's name? How can you pass the share along? As I mentioned earlier, getting the first share is a pain the first time, but then it becomes easier. Well the same is true with selling (or trading) your share. You can skip the rest of this chapter until you've gone through the steps of buying your first share. Then come back to it and read about how to sell your share when you're ready to do that. When you're ready, here's how it's done:

1) Make an agreement through the exchange board (the same way you did with the original share pur-

chase — agreeing on the closing share price of a certain share at a specified date).

2) Receive and deposit their cheque (for the agreed upon share price plus the $10 courtesy "fee".

3) Wait for their cheque to clear.

4) Find out *the exact* name the other person wants you to register the share in and fill out the "Transfer of Ownership" section on the back of the share certificate. Complete this section when you bring the certificate to the bank to get a signature guarantee.

At your bank you will tell them you need a signature guarantee. Explain you need a stamp *for securities transfers*. Some of the bank employees might not know about this, but you can usually find someone who does. Once you have the person who can guarantee your signature, fill out the back section marked "Transfer of ownership" and get the signature guarantee. Now you have to fill this out in front of the bank officer. Once you've done this, send the share certificate to the person who requested it. Mission accomplished.

Whether you pay the fees for the convenience of using a discount broker or spend virtually nothing to get your first share through an exchange board — it's not going to make a huge difference in the long-term. The key is to buy a share in a *quality* company and enrol in the DRIP/SPP. Then simply invest some money regularly (or whenever you can afford to) and gradually build up your portfolio.

Your wealth will grow automatically over time. And you will not have to pay any fees to keep things going. Every dollar is kept in *your* account adding and compounding and working to make *you* wealthier over time. It's not a widely publicized route and as such there will be some bank employees who don't understand what you're doing. Be patient and you will find someone there who can help you. This is an investing strategy that's not widely promoted because no companies have a vested interest in losing the fees you've been paying them. The next chapter will look at what you can do once your DRIP and SPP plan has been established for a while.

> ****Note** If you run into roadblocks on your quest for your first share, go to *www.dripinvesting.org* and explain the issue you've encountered. There are many experienced DRIP-pers there who can share their knowledge and help you.

10

MOVING UP TO THE "BIG LEAGUES"

"Money is plentiful for those who understand the simple laws which govern its acquisition."

■ **George Clason**

The main thrust of this book is that pretty much *anybody* without extensive investment knowledge (and between $50 and $100) can start on their journey to financial freedom. Once you've enrolled in the DRIP and SPP, gradual wealth accumulation becomes automatic. You can systematically add new stocks to your portfolio over time and participate in their DRIPs and SPPs. However, this would not be the final destination for me.

Once you've built up a sizeable position in a number of companies (perhaps at least a few hundred shares in about five or six companies) and you've started investing more money every month, you can then consolidate your holdings and open a discount brokerage account.

Why would you do this? You're probably thinking about how I spent the first part of the book attacking the financial industry as a mechanism that gradually sucks wealth from investors in the form of various fees or commissions and yet now I'm advocating "going over to the dark side" and investing your money with a broker?

The key advantage of following the DRIP/SPP strategy is that you need very little money or knowledge to get started. If you are content DRIPping, you can continue doing that forever. However, if your portfolio and knowledge have increased, going the brokerage route offers certain advantages. Once your portfolio is large enough ($50,000–$100,000), the number of available stocks you can invest in increases and you can build a stronger, more diversified portfolio. You can broaden your investment horizons and have more stocks from various industries to choose from because you can now include companies that might not offer DRIPs or SPPs. Buying US stocks is also made easier. In addition, all stock purchases are now instantaneous — no more hoops to jump through. You also receive one consolidated statement which makes it easier to track your portfolio. In addition, once you've reached the stage where you're dealing with larger sums of money, the various fees and commissions charged are not as important. I'll explain this with a brief example:

Suppose when you start investing, you only have enough to buy one share each month. The commission rate is $29 to purchase 1 to 1,000 shares. In the beginning you would be paying $29 *per share*! That's why DRIPs and SPPs are so useful — they allow you to avoid these commissions and that money you *would have* paid in fees and commissions gets directed into *your* portfolio and helps you accumulate *your own* wealth. However, after you've been investing for a while you will reach a stage where you are buying perhaps 100 shares at a time. In this case, the commission is still $29 total but since you are buying 100 shares, you are now paying only ($29 / 100) = 29 cents *per share*. Your costs *per share* to make purchases through a broker have dropped 99%. At some point the convenience of having a discount brokerage account outweighs the costs.

We quickly covered opening a brokerage account in the last chapter, but I want to go over it in a little more detail here:

1) Contact the major banks and get information on their discount brokers (all of them have one).
2) Compare the various services and fees they charge.
3) Choose one broker and contact them to find out how to open an account.

When you're opening the account, they will ask whether you want a "cash" account or "margin" account. A cash account is simply a regular account where you deposit money into the account over time and make sure you have enough money in your account to cover any stock or bond purchases you'd like to make.

With a margin account you can borrow money against your stocks and bonds to make purchases. In this case the brokerage can lend you money (usually at around prime or slightly higher) against the stocks you already own (sort of like a mortgage on your stocks). The problem is that if there is a stock market crash, you could get a "margin call". This means the broker asks you to put more money into the account or else they'll start selling some of your stocks to make sure they don't lose *their* money. This is kind of like foreclosing on your house if you stop making the mortgage payments. Generally, margin investing is a risky way to invest and I wouldn't recommend it for novice investors.

Once you've opened your brokerage account you need to get all your different holdings transferred into this account. Here's how you do this:

1) Contact the transfer agent(s) and ask them for the share certificates of your various companies for the number of shares you now own.

   Note It might not be in your interest to get *all* the shares in certificate form. In most cases if you keep at least one share with the transfer agent you can still participate in the DRIP and SPP. You'll be consolidating most of your holdings in the brokerage account, but by leaving a small amount with the transfer agent you'll keep your options open if you also want to continue DRIPping. In addition, brokerages won't accept fractional shares into your account.

2) Once you receive the certificates, go to your brokerage (or the bank that owns it) and tell them you'd like

to deposit the shares into your brokerage account.

It usually takes 3–5 business days for your shares to appear in your brokerage account. After you have done this with all your holdings, you will have a consolidated portfolio "under one roof".

This final step puts you on track for your final goal — financial freedom! These dividends keep getting paid — but now you receive them in cash. You can look for opportunities to add more shares of different companies when the price is cheap following the criteria I outlined in my first book, "*STOP WORKING: Here's How You Can!*". The next chapter will get into exactly what "financial freedom" is and show you when you've reached this point.

11

HOW DO YOU KNOW WHEN YOU'RE "FINANCIALLY FREE"?

"Money is better than poverty,
if only for financial reasons. "

 Woody Allen

The previous chapters have outlined how you can work towards financial freedom starting with a simple strategy and no investment knowledge. This chapter will explain how you can calculate when you've reached financial freedom. You don't have to do any of this planning until your investment strategy has been established — so if you're just getting started, feel free to skip this chapter and come back to it later. If you're ready to tackle the final step on your journey, read on.

How would you define financial freedom? Is it having a million dollars? How about two million?

A lot of the information you will hear with regards to retirement planning or financial freedom will focus on a certain fixed amount you need to accumulate to reach your goals. This sort of approach serves the interest of the financial industry in a number of ways — mostly by forcing you into accumulating wealth for as long as possible (and in the process creating fees for the industry).

Here's the definition I would use to decide when you've reached financial freedom:

Financial freedom is obtained when you can enjoy the standard of living <u>you want</u> without having to rely on <u>actively earned</u> income.

Once your investment income (dividends) reaches a point where you can afford the lifestyle you want — forever, you have reached financial freedom. Regardless of how you spend your time, the bills still get paid. This is an important point you need to understand — financial freedom means having the *income* you need to live the life you want. It's not a fixed amount of accumulated wealth.

Here are a few steps you can follow to estimate how much passive investment income you will need to reach financial freedom:

1. Take your current income and subtract all your "working-related" expenses.

Once you are relying on investment income, a lot of your working expenses will simply "disappear". Here are some possible expenses that "vanish" once you stop working for a living: CPP, EI, union dues, professional dues, commuting costs, child care, dry cleaning, business clothing costs, parking, coffee break expenses...

In addition, once you are relying on passive dividend income, you no longer have to save for retirement. Therefore, your pension plan or RRSP costs also "disappear".

2. Adjust your income needs to account for the fact that your income taxes will decrease as you earn Canadian dividend income instead of employment income.

Since passive dividend income from Canadian companies receive favourable tax treatment, your income tax bill should decrease *substantially*. An interesting fact I found in *"The Little Tax Fact Book"* provided by Ed Arbuckle from *Personal Wealth Strategies (www.finplans.net)* is that if all your income comes from eligible Canadian dividends, you can earn up to $46,345 without paying a cent in federal income tax! This figure applies to Ontario taxpayers in 2006, but the basic idea is that these dividends attract very little tax. This means that the amount of dividend income you need to sustain your desired lifestyle will be much lower than your current working income.

Remember:

By NOT working for money, but having money work for you, your income tax bill will go down (along with all your work-related expenses)!

It's also important to remember that this tax benefit only applies to dividends earned *outside* an RRSP.

After you've done these calculations you will have an amount that you need to earn in dividend income to achieve financial freedom while maintaining your current lifestyle. If it is difficult to do the tax calculations, you can seek assistance from an accountant or financial planner.

From personal experience, I figured I needed about *half* the amount of dividend income to match working income — but this might vary somewhat for you.

In many cases, you might only need half your current working income to be earned as passive dividend income to enjoy the same standard of living!

If you want to increase your standard of living, figure out how much more it will cost you and add that extra amount to the total you calculated above.

Once you've calculated how much you need, simply:

Keep investing until the amount of dividends generated from your portfolio equals the amount you calculated you need (from above).

Once you've reached your goal, you should be protected from gradually rising costs over time because the excellent companies you have invested in gradually increase their dividends along with inflation. You are now financially free to do whatever you want while your bills still get paid — automatically. The next chapter will focus on finding the money you'll need to start saving today so that you can implement this investing strategy.

12

FINDING THE MONEY... BEING FRUGAL VS. BEING CHEAP!

"My problem lies in reconciling my gross habits with my net income."

■ **Errol Flynn**

How can you find the money to invest when you feel like you are financially stretched to the limit already? Many people simply don't have a lot of extra money waiting to be invested. This chapter will give you some ideas for "finding" the money to start your investment program — even if the starting amount is modest.

I've read many financial or investing books that emphasize how forgoing simple small items such as avoiding coffee at Starbucks can lead to huge amounts of money over time. To me this advice is unhelpful for a few reasons. For starters, I don't drink coffee so this tip is not useful for me. However, the main reason I don't like this advice is that if you enjoy something, why would you want to give it up? Sure, if you want to live the miserly existence of

Ebenezer Scrooge you can become quite wealthy, but so what! What kind of life would that be? Being cheap is not my idea of successful financial freedom!

Saving money by being cheap is no fun, so don't worry — I won't try to convince you to do without.

Having said that, this chapter will focus on how you can spend money more economically — one of the fundamental aspects of achieving financial independence. I was rereading one of my favourite books the other week, "The Millionaire Next Door" which outlines some common characteristics of millionaires in the US. A feeling of pride came over me as I read the part about how the "thrifty Scots" make up only 1.7% of all households yet account for 9.3% of millionaires! It was interesting to note that most of the groups that were overrepresented with millionaires earned a higher income than the average of the other groups. The Scots were the exception — not earning a higher income, but nonetheless having a higher percentage of millionaires.

My family ancestry is mostly Scottish and I consider myself somewhat frugal. This approach was indeed passed down to me — mostly from my father, who definitely learned it from my grandfather. Discussing "money saving" is not as fun as thinking about investing, but it's a very important factor in reaching financial freedom. Remember each dollar you *save* is equivalent to working to *earn* around two dollars because when you work to earn money you have to pay all the costs associated with working such as income tax, CPP, EI, commuting costs, childcare, ... Although I don't make detailed budgets (I'd rather watch paint dry), I have created a simple framework for spending money. Basically, I divide my spending into "life-enhancing" and "non life-enhancing". I don't scrimp on the "life-enhancing" expenses because these are expenses which give me pleasure. But I watch "non life-enhancing" expenses like a hawk and try to minimize them. This approach focuses on spending smarter rather than working harder.

An example of a "non life-enhancing" expense would be taxes. Regardless of how much I personally pay in income taxes, I'm still entitled to the same level of services. There are no special schools or hospitals for higher tax payers! I will use every legal means possible to reduce my tax bill. For example, by earning Canadian based dividend income rather than employment income, I save a lot of income tax. As we saw in the last chapter, dividend income is very lightly taxed in Canada, whereas working income is the most heavily taxed income there is. In addition, dividend income avoids indirect taxes such as CPP and EI. Many people are in the position to reduce the taxes they pay by making a few simple adjustments. For example, by earning dividend income rather than interest income (as discussed earlier), or by simply making sure you claim all allowable deductions can make a huge difference to you tax bill.

Not spending money on things that don't bring you any pleasure is painless — and in many cases quite possible.

Minimizing these expenses which don't enhance your quality of life is simply being frugal. A lot of people read that word and feel it carries negative connotations. They feel it means "doing without" and let's face it, who wants to do that? A quick look in the dictionary gives the definition, "economical in use or expenditure, prudently saving or sparing, not wasteful"

The last part is the key — not wasteful! For example, I know one of the Canadian pastimes is complaining about the fees the banks charge (unless you're a bank shareholder), but the solution seems simple to me — if you don't want to be gouged $2 or whatever, only use your own banks' ATMs!

Being frugal (not wasteful) is a huge help in reaching financial freedom without depriving yourself.

What about buying the proverbial "umbrella on a sunny day"? I've seen this example for stocks — try to buy what's out of favour. How about also applying this idea in day-to-day life? For example, the beginning of winter in Ontario in 2006 brought very little snow such that retailers were discounting snow blowers and winter clothing in mid-January (where you could still see grass here in Ottawa)! My wife noticed all sorts of winter boots on sale — regularly $49.95, for $29.95 — a 40% discount. So she bought next year's boots for the kids and saved 40%. I challenge anyone to find an investment yielding a 40% tax-free, risk-free rate of return in the stock market (or anywhere else).

One quick note is that most times you see something "on sale", it's a phantom sale. Clothing stores are notorious for having year-round sales such that you're not really getting a bargain — but in this case it was a legitimate sale. This is a small dollar savings, but done repeatedly it can really add up.

Applying frugality to our annual trip to warmer climes also yielded some savings. In 2006 we booked a 2-bedroom condo in Orlando, Florida which cost $420 for a week through a special deal. The following year we were going to book the same 2-bedroom Condo for $480 US for the week, but a quick search of the internet led us to a better deal. Here it is....

We found a condo unit complete with a full kitchen, in-unit washer and dryer, living room, dining room, washroom, and loft-style bedroom with a king-sized bed, massive walk-in closet, and huge whirlpool tub and second bathroom on a resort setting with a heated pool, outdoor hot tub, tennis courts, basketball courts, free kids activities, a movie night with free popcorn, fenced and surrounded with mature oak trees for...$150 US for the week! This was an incredible deal for $25/night! What was the catch? We listened to a two-hour timeshare presentation which offered a free breakfast and free child care for the kids. When we looked at the numbers, we told the guy we weren't interested and that was it. So we saved $330 US or 69% for doing a quick search. Do you know of any investment that yields a tax-free, risk-free return of 69% in a week?

The internet has transferred power to the consumers. You can price compare with a click of the mouse and save a lot of money.

Being frugal doesn't mean buying the cheapest thing to save a few bucks — but getting the quality you want at a better price. An example is when we bought our family minivan. We looked at all types of vans and read the consumer reports and decided we wanted the Toyota Sienna rather than a lot of the other cheaper models available. The domestic companies had loads of incentives, but we liked the comfort, safety, and quality of the Toyota, so that's what we decided on. We went into a dealership and tried to negotiate a little on price near the end of the year as we figured they'd want to unload the last of that year's models…no deal, they wouldn't budge at all. We went to another dealer who had five of that year's model left in stock. It seems Toyota dealers won't negotiate much, but we did get $1200 off and also a much cheaper price on rust-proofing and window tinting (large profit margin items for the dealership).

Another example of frugality I'll mention was the in selling our house. Recently, my family has grown to four children — so we decided we needed a much bigger house, which we found and agreed to buy. We asked for a long closing so we would have a lot of time to sell our house. We were selling our condo townhouse for around $200,000, so real estate fees would amount to 5% or $10,000. In Ottawa, there is a company that operates a huge website and provides the materials to sell your house yourself for around $350 — so we decided to try that option. We sold our house fairly quickly and saved over $9,500. The result was the same — we sold our house, but we did it with a little effort on our part and saved a lot.

Some things can be done yourself with huge savings.

What about buying a house? When my family returned from Korea a few years ago, our condo townhouse in Ottawa was under a long-term lease, so we decided to try Wasaga Beach for a while. We could have rented, but the idea of paying $1,300 or more a month didn't appeal to me, so we looked into buying something. Since the beach had become a retirement area for many, there were countless similar bungalows we looked at. Demographically, Wasaga Beach is the right place for the retiring boomers, so we felt confident that if we didn't like life there, we would have no difficulty selling a bungalow — so off we went searching.

We saw many houses that seemed pretty similar and then we stumbled upon one that was owned as a rental property by a lady in the Toronto area. The place had been vacant for a few months and as we pulled up it looked terrible because the grass had not been watered all summer (since the beach is mostly sand, the grass dies quickly there). It had absolutely no curb appeal. Inside it was empty, and empty houses never look as good as furnished ones (that's why model homes always have some furnishings in them). The basic house was as good as any others we had seen; in fact the finished basement and back deck were better than many and it had been freshly painted. It was priced in the same range as the other houses we had seen, but with dead grass and the fact it was totally deserted, it just wasn't as aesthetically appealing.

All the bungalows similar to this one were selling for around $189,000–$195,000 at that time. We contacted the listing agent directly and told her she could be the selling agent as well as the listing agent (that way she would get commission from both sides of the transaction and be more interested in having *our* offer accepted). We then told her the house looked terrible and that we were only interested if the absent owners were somewhat motivated to sell, and offered $160,000. She said our offer was unrealistic and I agreed but mentioned that I'd have to see some movement on the other party's part or else we weren't interested. I also told her that if they did accept our offer, we would have no conditions attached and we could take possession immediately (we were staying at a motel, but the owner also wanted to stop paying taxes for a vacant property). We went back and forth and finally agreed to $179,000.

It wasn't the deal of a century, but after two weeks of fairly regular watering and moving some furniture in, the place would have easily sold in the $190,000–$195,000

range. We had saved more than $10,000 by finding some-
thing that was essentially just as good, but didn't look
pleasing. Isn't that also the key to stock investing?

*Sometimes you can save by buying a "diamond in the rough"
rather than the sparkling diamond. Then use a little effort
to remove the "rough".*

The few savings I listed above amounts to over $20,000
— definitely worth the little bit of extra effort. These savings occurred a few years ago when I was in my mid-thirties,
so if I took this money and invested it at 10% (the long-term
average return of the stock markets) until 65 (the "retirement age" for many), it would grow to almost **$350,000**.

*A little effort expended towards more efficient spending can
yield enormous results.*

The point is not to be a miser — what kind of lifestyle
would that be? The point is that a little thought can lead
to big savings — without any compromise to your lifestyle.
I understand that many people lead very busy lives, so
you'll have to find your spots where the extra effort is
worth the money — in some cases it may not be.

I know this is considered boring advice by many —
investing is much more interesting to most people, but as
shown, the results can be huge. In most cases, the savings
are a much higher rate of return than most of your investments — and they're usually risk-free and tax-free. This
spending approach can really help you find the extra

money to contribute to your financial freedom. So take a page from the "thrifty Scots". I assure you that it will be worth the effort.

The next section of this book is dedicated to teaching children about money and getting them started on their road to financial freedom. If this does not apply to you, skip to the last chapter and then get started. Your financial freedom is within grasp — so go get it.

SECTION II

Your Kids and Money

13

DEMOGRAPHICS AS DESTINY!

*"For the hand that rocks the cradle —
Is the hand that rules the world"*

William Ross Wallace

A great book by the name of *"Boom, Bust, Echo"* by David Foot first ignited my interest in demographics. Initially, this interest was one additional factor to consider when researching possible investments. For example, as the baby boomers began to focus on retirement planning in the 1990s, demand for investment products such as mutual funds exploded. The result is that companies that offered these products were great investments. In the future, demand for medical products and services should increase as this large population cohort become seniors. Gradually I came to view demographics as a powerful force that has a huge impact on everything. Simply put, in many ways, demographics is destiny.

For example, let's look at Japan. Japan has the oldest population in the history of our planet — it's essentially the geriatric ward of the world! But...do you remember the 1980's when Japan was set to dominate every industry. I started university in 1989 and my major was Business, so I remember some courses discussing how the Japanese were accomplishing incredible manufacturing feats. "Americans" (read most of the western world), were lazy and complacent and simply couldn't compete with the Japanese. Gradually Toyotas and Hondas replaced GM and Fords on the roads. Politicians wrung their hands and complained that Japan was happy to export to our open markets, but kept their markets closed to our products. Every week carried a different announcement — like when the Japanese bought a controlling interest in the Rockefeller Centre. Even Hollywood got into the act. I remember in the movie "*Back to the Future II*" the character of Marty (Michael J. Fox) does something against company policy and he is fired by his Japanese boss — the message being that in the future the Japanese would dominate every domain. Some people even thought Japanese would replace English as the world's business language.

During the 1980s, a large part of the Japanese population was entering their most productive years — which helped their economy immensely. Many people talked about how the "Japanese business model" was so much better than the American one at producing the best quality goods. Quickly Japan proceeded to become an economic powerhouse. Then irrational exuberance swept over the entire country. This craziness reached a point where in

1989, it was calculated that the land value of the imperial palace in the heart of Tokyo was greater than all the land in California!

The Nikkei indexed raced ahead year after year. The Nikkei index is a collection of the major corporations of Japan — similar to the TSX here in Canada. The number reflects how the share prices are doing (the higher the number on the index, the higher the general share prices). The Nikkei index peaked on December 29, 1989 at 38,915 points. At the time of this writing (18 years later) the Nikkei index sits at around 17,000. In other words if you had invested in the Nikkei index when I started university in 1989, (while the professors in my Commerce courses were discussing the invincibility of the Japanese production model), your net return over 18 years would be minus 56%!

What happened? Why has Japan struggled with an almost 20 year recession? There are a lot of factors at play, but a large part of the explanation rests with the fact that Japan has the oldest population in the history of the world — and that their old-age population continues to grow. This factor has dragged down their economy.

How about here in Canada? How does our situation look in the future? How about the future of those born after the baby boomers?

Basically when one looks at demographics, an extremely important factor is the fertility rate (the average number of children each woman has). I'm not a demographics expert, but if you look up "Canadian declining fertility" on Google, you get an interesting picture of where things are headed. The "replacement" fertility rate (the rate at which a population neither grows nor shrinks over the long-term) is 2.1. In other words, all the women must have an average of 2.1 kids for the population to remain stable (2 to replace the parents and another 0.1 to make up for premature deaths). Canada currently has a rate of around 1.5. In other words, without immigration Canada loses 25% of its population with each successive generation.

The wild card for Canada is that it has the highest per capita immigration rate in the world. This will slow but not stop our aging population — requiring more government funding and providing less tax revenue.

So what? What's the point of addressing demographics?

Well, there are a number of factors that come into play. With the risk of being labelled a cynic and contradicting what our politicians have been telling us, longer-term I don't trust the sustainability of the Canada Pension Plan, Old Age Security, and Universal Health Care. I've heard the politicians claim everything has been fixed and we'll all be okay, but I remain very sceptical.

The simple reality is that for young people today, these programs can't be relied upon and will be more difficult to sustain in the future. The year 2007 was the year in which the first Baby Boomers in Canada started turning 60 — and this is just the beginning. With more retirees and fewer workers going forward, I don't feel these programs will continue in their current form. Some medical procedures that used to be funded by the provinces no longer are. University tuitions have risen quickly as governments have cut back on funding. User fees are being added to various services. In the US, the age you can collect social security is creeping up. Here in Canada, the government instead decided to raise CPP premiums — but I'm doubtful that the problem is totally "solved". The government has had ten years of budget surpluses but this will not continue once most of the baby boomers have reached retirement and become recipients of government money rather than contributors through taxes. Add to this the fact that recent immigrants are doing much more poorly financially than previous immigrants — so immigration (although helpful), won't solve the problem.

The point is that if you hope for a secure future for your children, you will have to take some action on your own. The first part of this book has detailed how *you* can start an investment plan for under $100. The following chapters will use that strategy to explain how to implement a solid plan for your children while at the same time teaching them financial knowledge — something sorely lacking in our schools. The old idea of simply getting a good education and then finding a great career job is becoming more difficult. Having a strong knowledge of money matters will become imperative for young people as time goes by. Social programs are based on the assumption of ever more people funding the programs. As we move towards an inverted population pyramid, where each successive generation is *smaller* than the previous one, these programs will be stretched financially. The solution will be for individuals to pick up the slack — something we're already witnessing. I hope this section can help lay a solid financial foundation for your children.

14

YOU CAN'T LEARN TO RIDE A BIKE IF YOU NEVER FALL DOWN

"Wealth Never Survives Three Generations"
■ **Ancient Chinese Adage**

The above Chinese quote caught my attention. The North American version is "Shirtsleeves to shirtsleeves in three generations", but the principle is the same. Why is it that family wealth is often squandered in subsequent generations? How can you teach your children financial intelligence? I think part of the answer lies in the idea that you can't *tell* children how to ride a bike — they have to learn it for themselves by falling down a few times. Wouldn't it make sense to follow the same line of thinking with regards to money? If you give people responsibility, you will often be pleasantly surprised with what they'll accomplish.

For example, when I started university my dad offered to pay it all for me. I remember going to the bookstore with a blank cheque in hand and buying all my books. It's interesting that I didn't search for used books that might have been cheaper — I just bought them all at once. I also bought many optional books that were listed. The next year my dad's financial situation had worsened. Business was not good and Canada had entered the recession of the early 1990s. I paid my own way through school for the final three years. Now that I was paying the bills, I became much more frugal. When buying books I examined each one carefully and only bought the ones I felt I needed. I did many courses without ever buying the book, or shared with other students. It was amazing how having to pay for my own books while earning $5.40/hour changed my perspective on things.

In the book, *The Millionaire Next Door*, which I mentioned earlier, Thomas Stanley and William Danko explain how the spending habits of the "typical" millionaire are very different from the stereotypical image people have of millionaires. The book highlights the fact that a lot of people with substantial wealth live a frugal lifestyle. It also goes on to explain how children of many wealthy people who over-indulge their children end up creating people who are financially dependent on their parents. The children were never forced to learn good money habits — so they never did.

As mentioned earlier, I don't believe in budgeting but instead divide expenses into life-enhancing (a nice vacation, a new car, meals out) and non life-enhancing (income taxes, work-related expenses, interest charges). I didn't want to deny myself to reach financial security but I also am vigilant in eliminating expenses that don't add value to my life. These are the lessons I would like to pass onto my children.

So how do you get children to spend money more efficiently? Simple — let them make financial decisions. It's almost guaranteed that they'll make some mistakes from time to time, but mistakes are effective learning tools. It's better for them to make the small money mistakes while they're young than when they're older (and the mistakes are more expensive).

I disagree with the "guidance" (I call it financial coercion) that many "teach you kids about money" books espouse. I've read a number of these books and a lot of them support the idea of giving your child an allowance and then forcing them to put 10% toward charity, 10% toward long-term goals, 10% saving, ... In my opinion, the idea of giving kids money is so that *they* can manage it. It should be *their* money. Guidance should be just that — advice — and not a forced plan.

Let kids do what they want with their own money — and let them make mistakes and feel the consequences. A mistake is an infinitely better tool for teaching than a parent engaged in infinite preaching!

By giving responsibility to your children gradually and letting them feel the natural consequences of their actions, you are teaching them a very valuable lesson. Hopefully by making the mistakes when they're young, they'll avoid some of these same mistakes when they're older.

How about allowances? I don't give any directly. This sounds strange but let me explain.

The main issue I have with giving an allowance is the overall message it conveys. What's the message that's transmitted to our children from a pretty early age? The traditional idea of "study hard, get good grades, then go to university and get a good career" is ingrained. In most instances, the "good career" is the end point of this line of thinking. That's not the message I want to convey to my children. The idea of studying hard to get a good job has merit, but it's just a starting point. The end point in my opinion is to obtain financial freedom — to be free from having to rely on a paycheque so that you have the time to pursue your interests. This doesn't mean you have to stop working — it just means that you have more options. You can choose work that might not be as high-paying but offers other intangible rewards without worrying about the financial consequences.

Again — how do most wealthy people achieve financial independence? Not through getting a good job but by becoming an owner of wonderful businesses. This can be achieved through stock investments. The richest people aren't employees — they're owners. Working for a living is more difficult in the long-run than investing for a living. Employees pay much more tax than investors and are more affected by the ups and downs of the economy. Ownership is where the goodies are! I feel investing should be given equal emphasis along with the traditional idea of choosing a good career — the two ideas are not mutually exclusive.

I want to gradually get my children to start thinking along the lines of investing as well as pursuing a good career. Rather than giving an allowance every week I bought my children some shares and income trusts which pay dividends on a regular basis. The idea is that the kids learn that another great way to earn income is through ownership of stocks. They have an ownership in an actual enterprise that they can see and feel they are a part of. They can get interested in how *their* company is doing. It also reinforces wise spending as I am not going to forward any money to them after they've spent their own, so the dividend cheque has to last them a while as these payments don't arrive every week. They'll also learn over time that the dividends rise (at least for great companies), so that they're getting raises on a regular basis. They will also get a copy of the annual report every year updating them on what's been happening with their business. They can go to the annual meetings and ask questions of the top management and get the free snacks offered. They become a part of the companies that provide the goods and services we all use. This is all a gradual learning process that will become more involved as they get older.

In addition to all the above, there is one extremely important lesson children should learn about with financial teachings — control over their emotions with regards to investing. With the risk of sounding like a broken record — investing is 90% emotion and 10% intelligence. When I speak publicly I'm amazed at all the people who are obsessed with the ups and downs of the market. Many people are using a casino-like mentality trying to buy and sell to make money. The financial media has a short-term focus where the daily action of the market is hyped. Since the shares represent their "allowance", they won't be tempted to sell in a panic when the stock price falls. They'll be focused on the cash coming to them on a regular basis — which is the cornerstone of my investing philosophy. This is the factor that allows investors to become financially free without being held captive to the stock market. It's this lesson I want to pass on. As the old adage goes:

> Give a man a fish and you feed him for a day. Teach a man to fish and you feed him for a lifetime.

If your children learn not to worry about short-term volatility in stock markets (a lesson that many seasoned investors *still* have never learned), they will be well on their way to obtaining financial independence.

But how do you do this? How do you pass on the knowledge of proper investing to your kids? Even more difficult, how do you teach them proper investing when your own track record is limited or you don't have a large sum of money to get them started?

Once again the idea of DRIPs and SPPs offer a powerful tool you can use to get your children interested in investing and start them on the road to financial freedom. The advantage of this approach is that you can start this plan with a fairly small sum of money and add to it whenever any extra money is available. Once your children get part-time jobs, they also have an efficient place where they can direct some of their savings.

The next chapter will give you some ideas for creating a solid financial foundation for your children and teach them some important (and often neglected) lessons that they will not learn in the school system.

15

GIVING YOUR CHILDREN THE TOOLS THEY'LL NEED

"One generation plants the trees; another gets the shade"

■ **Chinese Proverb**

In this chapter I am going to explain a strategy of how to set up your children on course for financial freedom at a young age. I understand that some people might not have extra money available to invest on their children's behalf — so a small start by setting up DRIPs and SPPs would be the answer. Once the amount invested has grown (or if you already have some money to invest for your children), this chapter will give you an idea of how to implement a solid plan.

The first step in the process is choosing some securities that you feel comfortable holding for the long-term. When you initially give your children securities, there are some issues which you must consider before you go about it. Basically, there are a few main options. You can register the certificates in the kids' names directly, create an informal "in trust" account at your brokerage, or create a formal trust with a lawyer. I will not get into formal trusts as they are too complex and expensive to set up to serve the purposes outlined here and they are beyond the scope of this book.

The informal trust route involves opening an account "in trust" with your broker. Within this account, you can buy various securities and reinvest dividends to a certain extent. The one important fact is that you usually can't invest partial shares and the extra money simply gets converted to cash. The advantages of this type of account include more flexibility when selling shares. If you buy share certificates directly in your child's name, they become very difficult to sell before the child reaches the age of majority. In addition, if your child decides to blow the money you've saved for him/her on a new car after turning 18, there is not much you can do. We'll get into the informal trust route in more detail in the next chapter.

I opted for getting physical share certificates in my children's names directly. I wanted it to be absolutely clear to them that these were *their* shares, not mine. I also set up the DRIPs through the transfer agents. Implementing all this was the focus of the first section of this book. This route allows them to acquire partial shares — which is a huge benefit. All the dividends are reinvested every quarter. They possess a physical certificate and can see their investment. They can stop by the bank they own or the retail store and analyze how they think it's being run. They can go to the annual meeting and ask questions.

More importantly, they can't sell their shares for a number of years so they are committed to being like real *owners* of the business rather than simply *traders* of a ticker symbol. Over time, they'll see first hand that market corrections are the friend of the patient investor because when the market plummets, their dividends will purchase more shares for them. They can also get used to the idea that money can come from *ownership of a business* rather than *only* from working. If you start investing for your children early, they have many years to get used to the idea that stocks are long-term investments that bear "fruit" in the form of regular (preferably rising) dividends over time. This is an important lesson that I want to pass onto my children.

The investment strategy I use follows certain criteria. Most stocks are not worth owning at any price — over 95% of them should be avoided. You should focus on companies that offer a product or service that is recession-proof, a company that is preferably the number one player in their industry with a long history of performance and a record of consistent dividend payments (and preferably rising dividends). If you currently don't have a few thousand dollars to invest for your children, enrol them in DRIPs and SPPs (following the plan of getting the first share outlined in section one) to get them started and build it up over time. For those of you who do have a few thousand dollars to create an investment plan for your children, I'm going to go over the strategy I've used to give you some possible ideas.

I created a starting portfolio for my children as follows:

50 shares in RBC Financial Group
50 shares in George Weston Ltd.
100 shares of Pengrowth energy trust
10 shares of Enbridge Inc

The portfolio above represented a fairly large initial investment (around $8,500) to start. My intention is to not add anything to my kids' portfolio from this point onward. You will also see later on that I have no intention of saving huge amounts of money to pay for their education — so from that perspective it's a one-time gift that should cover all future "allowances" and their "education money".

So here's how I set everything up. RBC Financial Group (which in reality is Royal Bank) is the largest bank in Canada and has been operating since 1864. Historically, RBC has managed to raise its dividend regularly and I see no reason why it shouldn't continue doing so. It's well positioned in the banking industry (which has been one of the most profitable industries in Canada for a long time). It also has a lot of growth potential in the US market where it's been gradually making acquisitions. Interestingly, most companies that operate in Canada are pipsqueaks compared to their US counterparts but because of the nature of how the banking industry evolved south of the border, our banks are pretty big compared to many US banks.

With this holding, I gave 50 shares to each of my children and immediately enrolled them in the DRIP. Now each dividend gets reinvested such that the number of shares they own gradually increases. I understand that 50 shares is not a huge stake, but with a decade or two of reinvestment and compounding, this holding will grow for them over time.

In addition, after each dividend is paid, I get a statement mailed to my house showing how much the dividend was and at what price it was reinvested. If history is any guide, there should be a few periods over the next decade or two where something happens to create pessimism in the company and drive down the stock price. As my children get older I hope to use these market corrections as a teaching tool to show them how stock market crashes are the friend of the long-term investor. As the market corrects and the price of RBC Financial goes down, their regular dividend will automatically buy more shares. When this happens, I hope to show them what factors are being reported in the media at that time that are responsible for the drop in stock prices.

The beauty of having the shares registered in their names is that it's very difficult to sell the shares (and impossible for minor children). This forces the whole "buy and hold" on them — even if their inclination would be to sell. Since the securities are actually in *their* name, they can see that the reduction in price is actually a reduction in *their* wealth. The point is to let them experience the real emotions one experiences in stock market declines. A few thousand dollars to a 10-year-old is like a few *hundred thousand* to an adult — so the emotional impact is the same.

Eventually as the pessimism subsides (as it usually does) and the share price returns to it's previous level, they'll see that the short-term panic that caused the price to fall was simply "noise" and hopefully they'll learn to ignore it. They'll have experienced the feeling of a down market without having the control to call their broker and issue the sell call. If my children can learn this, they'll be ahead of most investors before they are finished high school.

The next stock, Weston, has been one of my worst investments. I originally bought some shares for around $100 each and since then it's declined significantly to around $75/share at the time of writing. First the bakery part of the business was hit with the rise in popularity of the "Atkins" diet which advocated cutting carbohydrates from your diet. Then Wal-Mart stated that they intend to bring the superstore concept up to Canada and offer more groceries for sale. With this announcement, Loblaws (majority owned by Weston) sank. There is a lot of pessimism surrounding this stock, but rightly or wrongly I feel its longer-term performance should be solid.

George Weston Ltd is owned by the Weston family which happens to be the second richest family in Canada. Galen Weston and family ranked 59th in the world on the Forbes richest list in 2006. I usually don't mind riding on the coattails of billionaires when it comes to investing.

Weston was founded in 1882 and has become one of North America's largest food processing and distribution groups. I eat food. I like food. I can understand food. Weston is in the food business. In its annual report, I see that Weston operated 66 baking facilities across North America. It also operated 2 dairy facilities in Ontario. In addition to this, Weston owns a majority stake in the largest grocery retailer in Canada (Loblaws, Real Canadian Super-stores, Zehrs, No Frills, and many other banners). Through this ownership, they also control President's Choice — which is a highly respected food brand.

With Weston shares, there is no DRIP offered. They will simply mail out a small dividend cheque every quarter. The goal of this investment is to teach my children that people can earn money, but owning shares also earns money. Their small ownership in this company should provide them with a gradually rising dividend over the long-term that they're free to spend however they want. This dividend will be part of their "allowance". They can also see that regardless of the ups and downs of the stock market or the stock price, dividend payments are largely unaffected. They will also get a feeling of "ownership" when our family does the weekly grocery shopping.

The next investment is Pengrowth — which is an energy trust. Essentially, it pumps oil and gas out of the ground and sells it. Then with the money it earns, it sends cash to shareholders. The long-term viability of energy trusts is questionable with the tax changes to income trusts, but Pengrowth should continue to exist in some corporate form. The advantage here is that the yield is very high and the payments are made monthly. My goal here is to have a portion of the Pengrowth distribution deposited into the children's' bank account and then use these proceeds to purchase additional shares in the last holding — Enbridge. Regular contributions will be made through the Enbridge SPP — which has no minimum as mentioned earlier. They will also be enrolled in the DRIP. The other portion of the Pengrowth distribution can be spent by my kids — the other part of their "allowance".

Enbridge is a company I did not own in my own portfolio before getting my children started — but the fact that it is a solid company that offers a DRIP and SPP was a huge consideration when setting up my children's plan. The main factor that convinced me to add this company was that they could reinvest very small amounts of money over time. As mentioned earlier in this book, Enbridge operates pipelines and gas distribution mostly in Canada and the US (but with some international operations). Pipelines are good businesses as they ship either oil or gas which people need regardless of the state of the economy. If you go to the company website, you can see that over a 52 year period, Enbridge has delivered a stunning 13.3% annual return compared to an average of around 10% for Canadian markets as a whole. That might not seem like much of a difference, but if you invest $1,000 for 50 years at the different rates, here's what you get:

$1,000 invested for 50 years at 10%   = **$116,391**
$1,000 invested for 50 years at 13.3% = **$513,630**

So by investing in Enbridge instead of the market index, you'd earn over four times the money!

With this stock, I'd like to teach my kids about the power of DRIPs coupled with money directed through SPPs. Since oil and gas tends to be quite volatile, I would expect the distributions from Pengrowth to fluctuate — but this does not present a problem. They'll be able to decide where increased or decreased payouts should go — either spending or adding to their Enbridge shares.

With these stocks I'll be able to create a foundation for my children to learn about investing. Of course right now I control the whole process, but as they get older they will assume more responsibility. Hopefully they'll learn patience and control of their emotions over time and also have a long enough time frame to see the results of constant reinvestment. At the end of this process, when they attain the age of majority, they'll have their own nest egg started. My hope is that through the process of getting them started and experiencing the progress over time, they'll have a greater appreciation of how proper investing works. This is the type of financial lesson that is not offered anywhere else — but it is an important one. The next chapter will look at the legalities of buying your minor children shares.

16

"TRUST" YOUR MINOR CHILDREN

"The minute you read something that you can't understand, you can almost be sure that it was drawn up by a lawyer."

■ **Will Rogers**

This chapter is for anyone who wants to start a child or children with their own little portfolio even if it starts with just one share. After you've chosen a company (or companies) you'd like your children to own shares in, you must decide on the ownership structure. Setting this up for a minor child can be a little tricky.

As I mentioned in an earlier chapter, when you buy shares for your minor child, you have three options. You can register the shares in the name of the child directly, you can create an informal trust, or you can set up a formal trust. A formal trust is a legal entity that requires the use of a lawyer to set up and it carries with it certain costs. This would only be recommended for those with a *substantial* amount to invest and is beyond what we're examining on here, so we'll focus on the other two options.

If you register the shares in the name of a minor child directly, there are some disadvantages. First, it is very difficult to sell them (if not impossible). A quick discussion with a lawyer told me that you would have to get a legal opinion from a court that the arrangement was a "de facto" informal trust. I'm not a lawyer and a lot of this was beyond my understanding, but the basic idea I came away with was that it would be very difficult to sell the shares once you've bought them.

In addition, minors can't open checking accounts so this presents another set of problems as it becomes more difficult to add money through an SPP. There are stringent rules such that the first cheque is supposed to come from a bank account of the person who owns the share certificates. For minors you can sign a declaration stating that you are the legal guardian and then send in a cheque from your own account. Once you've sent in the first cheque, each subsequent payment can be from any bank account. These rules were implemented for anti-money laundering purposes. The only money my kids have ever laundered was when one of my sons found a nickel at the park and we forgot to empty his pockets prior to doing the weekly wash, but this requirement is stringently enforced.

One additional factor worth noting is that if you register the shares directly in the name of the child, the child has complete control as soon as he/she turns 18. You might not like the idea of coming home one day to find that the years of small contributions that have been made to your child's portfolio have been converted into a new sports car.

The other option is to create an informal trust. This is pretty simple as all you have to do is register the shares like this:

"Your Name" in trust for "Child's Name"

By doing this, you've given yourself the ability to sign any necessary documents which can cut down immensely on the potential headaches. In addition, with this arrangement, you also keep control which means you decide when and whether to turn the shares over to your children.

As shown in the last chapter, I registered the shares in my children's names directly for the reasons I mentioned. I liked the idea of them feeling a total sense of "ownership". With this feeling they can experience the full emotional impact of stock market volatility. However, for simplicity many people follow the informal trust route. This makes it much easier to legally control the holdings. Regardless of which path you choose, getting started is a good way to begin teaching the benefits of investing to your children. The next chapter will get into a huge issue many parents face — funding you children's post-secondary education through RESPs.

> ****Note** This book is not meant to be a tax guide. As already stated in the legal disclaimer at the front of this book, I am not a tax expert. However, there are certain tax-related issues you should be aware of when giving a gift to minor children.

When giving a gift to a minor child, all income (dividends — in the case of shares) is taxable in the hands of the person who gave the shares.

"Second-generation" income is taxed in the hands of the minor child. This means if the dividends (from above) are reinvested to buy more shares, the dividends earned on these new shares are taxed in the child's hands.

Capital Gains are also taxed in the hands of the child.

Investments purchased with money from the Child Tax Benefit or an inheritance are taxed exclusively in the name of the child. So use this money to build up their portfolio if you can.

If you set up an informal trust account, but then still use these funds for personal use, the Canada Revenue Agency might determine that you in fact are still the owner of this money and tax you accordingly. Therefore, once you've started a portfolio for your children, don't touch it!

**Legal Disclaimer I am not a tax expert. The above information might be inaccurate or incorrect and this information should not be relied upon. The reader must seek proper verification of tax information and its possible implications from an appropriate tax expert before initiating any investment strategy.

17

RESPs — ARE THEY A GOOD IDEA?

"If you want children to keep their feet on the ground, put some responsibility on their shoulders."

■ **Abigail Van Buren**

I vividly remember a presentation I was giving at the Financial Forum Show in Toronto. Generally I like to do quick presentations and then open things up for questions. I've always found interactive communication is better than one-way communication. During the question and answer, one person questioned whether I could stay retired with four children — wasn't the cost of their education going to bankrupt me? How much was I regularly contributing to their RESPs? RESPs stand for Registered Education Savings Plans and I'll explain how they work below.

I heard gasps when my first answer explained how I did not plan on funding most of my children's post-secondary education. Then strong disagreement was voiced when I mentioned that I did not own any RESPs for my kids. How could I not see the benefit of these plans — and not already be taking advantage of them?

I think the RESP has followed the RRSP as being over-hyped. These plans are presented in such a way that if you're not contributing to them, you are failing in this area. For RRSPs, senior citizens are shown in fast food uniforms and the message is that if you don't max out RRSPs, you're destined for destitution. For RESPs, photos of babies are shown and the message is to start saving ASAP. Combined with this tactic is the method of making investing out to be very complicated so that the only solution is to seek the advice of a "professional". I have a problem when fear is used in advertising to persuade people to act a certain way — whether it be avoiding poverty in retirement or broadening your kids' options for education.

Having said all that, RESPs are a pretty good deal. Here's how they work. You contribute after-tax dollars and the money grows tax-free until withdrawal. For each contribution you make up to $2,500 the federal government will contribute 20% extra (or up to $500). So for example, if you decided to contribute $2,000, the government would add (20% X $2,000) = $400. This extra money is called Canada Education Savings Grants. There is a lifetime limit of $50,000 that can be deposited for each child. Upon withdrawal, the money is taxed in the hands of the beneficiary — your university aged son or daughter. This arrangement usually results in little or no tax being paid because university students generally have low income and they can deduct education costs on their tax returns.

So with the benefits listed above, why would I not contribute to RESPs for my children? Everybody's situation is different, but I'll give you an explanation of my thinking and why I haven't started any RESPs yet.

One factor often ignored in RESP literature is the fact that they have some drawbacks. With the regular stock investments I've created for my children, there are no constraints. They can invest in any security and in any amount. The stocks will be taxed as dividend and capital gains income — which is favourable. In addition, there are little or no costs with DRIP plans whereas many RESP plans incur administrative fees every year.

In addition, I think the estimates of how much university will cost have been inflated — which helps the financial industry sell more investments within RESPs to worried parents. How much will university really cost and therefore how much do we really need to save?

If any of my children choose to go away to university, the cost per year (currently) is estimated around $15,000 — (I checked a local university estimate in addition to one created by the Ontario Undergraduate Student Alliance). So $15,000 would be the *highest* amount needed — and this amount includes entertainment and other incidentals. Students who choose to stay home would pay substantially less.

The minimum wage in Ontario is currently $8/hr (but is projected to rise to over $10/hour in the next few years). If a student worked part-time during the school year, (10–15 hours/week) they would earn around $100/week during that time or around $3,000 for the year. In the summer, they'd have maybe 16 weeks @ 40 hours/week or around $6,000. So every student should be able to earn at least $9,000 per year. This is assuming a low paying job and two weeks off during the summer and four weeks off during the school year (for exams). So by assuming high costs with low income, there would be a shortfall of ($15,000 cost–$9,000 income) = $6,000/year. I know that prices will rise over time, but so will wages. I also know that tuition increases have outpaced inflation over the last number of years with a massive decrease in post-secondary funding — but I don't think this scenario will be repeated as the major cuts to balance budgets have already been made.

This potential shortfall excludes the possibility that a higher paying summer job might be found. For instance, I found a summer job that paid me around $12/hour back in 1993. There are many co-op and other jobs students can get that offer reasonable rates of pay. In addition, by the time my kids reach university, there will be a labour shortage due to the retiring baby boomers, so they'll face a much better job market than I did.

This financial scenario also excludes any possible bursaries or scholarships — of which there are more than most people realize. It also ignores the fact that there are two large universities and a large college in Ottawa (where we live), so my children could choose to keep living at home and cut their costs immensely. Any number of these possibilities could cut the shortfall enormously or even eliminate it. I refuse to be herded into the "you better start maxing out your children's RESP as soon as they're born" camp.

The final reason that I personally haven't started saving through an RESP yet is that I want my children to shoulder a large part of the responsibility for their own education. By the time people reach 18 I think they should be somewhat financially independent. Learning financial lessons is equally important as what they'll learn at university.

I've already given them a portfolio of stocks that should increase over time. This money will be available to them. The difference here is that this is *their money* to do *whatever* they want with. If it was all in an RESP, it sort of says, "Here's your school money." As I strongly agree with the old assertion that, "Necessity is the mother of invention", I'm hoping my kids find a way to pay their own way through school while keeping their portfolios mostly intact. After years of seeing the reinvestments accumulating, I hope they'll have a better appreciation for how long it took to accumulate this money rather than simply receiving a "cheque from Mom and Dad" via an RESP every semester.

In addition, I remember when my family was living in Wasaga Beach; we knew another family who were not in the position to fund their son's university costs. He rolled up his sleeves and started his own landscaping business — which was quite successful. He earned enough money each summer to pay his expenses during the year. He attended university away from home and didn't have a regular part-time job during the school year. The choice of how my children decide to pay for their education will be theirs to make.

I know many people might disagree with me, but I feel by the time people gain rights that come with obtaining the age of majority, they should also have some responsibilities. I'm not saying I won't *ever* contribute to an RESP, because as we get closer to the time for my kids to go off to post-secondary school, I might be willing to help them a little more — but I won't pay it all for them. A few years of contributions could help eliminate the potential shortfall shown above without having to start saving while they're still in diapers. I also don't know how the whole education funding landscape will change over the next decade or more, so I'll start planning when I'm closer to that stage and have a clearer picture. Regardless, my children will have a large role to play in financing their own education.

Whether or not you decide to focus on RESPs is your personal choice. However, the next chapter will cover how *you might be eligible for a virtually free RESP* for your children.

18

WHEN YOU FIND FREE MONEY — TAKE IT!

"Education costs money, but then so does ignorance."

■ **Claus Moser**

All things being equal, I would much prefer to have money outside my RRSP, RESP, etc. then registered inside. However, when a situation comes along where it will cost you absolutely *nothing* to get free money — you should go for it. RESPs are widely advertised because there are certain advantages to them — but RESPs do require you to save some of your own money. This chapter will cover how you might be eligible for absolutely free money under a plan called the Canada Learning Bond.

To be eligible for this, your child must have been born after December 31, 2003 and you have to be receiving the National Child Benefit Supplement. Many people will not be eligible for this because your income has to be fairly low to qualify. The government of Canada website mentions that the family income usually has to be below $36,378 and this figure is adjusted every year. If this situation will never apply to you, feel free to skip to the next chapter.

However, even though this amount seems like a low threshold to some people, there are certain factors that can cause your income to go down in a given year. Circumstances could include if you take extended time off work in a given year, make a large "catch up" RRSP contribution, or start your own business to name a few possibilities.

If you are eligible for this benefit, you can set up an RESP and get $500 deposited into it without any of the money coming out of your own pocket. If you're eligible, here's exactly what you have to do to obtain it:

1. Make sure your child was born in 2004 or later (those born before 2004 are not eligible).
2. If you child is eligible, you need to get a Social Insurance Number for the child. You can Google "SIN card" to get the info on where to apply in your city.
3. Once you have the SIN card, open up an RESP account.

There are many avenues you can pursue, but the easiest way is to go to any major bank. If you open up an RESP and use the mutual funds offered by the bank (all major banks have their own funds), there should be no administrative fees — just double-check with them before opening the account. Many brokerage RESPs charge an annual fee of around $50/year for administering the plan, so if you are only contributing the free money from the Canada Learn-

ing Bond, it would work out to 10% of your original
investment every year.

> ****Note** You shouldn't have to deposit any money when opening
> the bank mutual fund RESP.

4. Once you've opened the RESP, the bank will apply for
   the Canada Learning Bond on your behalf.

> ****Note** The entire process should cost you nothing — and the
> bank handles all the paperwork.

Once all the above steps are taken, provided you've
met the criteria above, $500 will be deposited directly into
your child's RESP (and also an additional $25 will be sent
to cover the cost of opening the RESP, but you should be
able to open it without paying any fees). This money is tax-
free and it doesn't affect any other benefits you receive. In
addition, you will also get $100 extra for every year after
the initial year that you receive the National Child Benefit
Supplement. If your income rises to the point where you
are no longer eligible for this supplement every year, the
money that has already been deposited into your child's
RESP remains there — it's not taken back by the government. In total you can receive up to $2,000 per child
absolutely free. If your child doesn't go to post-secondary
education, this money is returned to the government. It
can't be used for other children.

Once the money is deposited into the RESP account and
you've chosen mutual funds to avoid the administrative fees

as mentioned above, you have to decide how you want to invest it. I would keep things simple and go for good quality companies that pay dividends by directing the money into a dividend fund. Over time this free money should grow — even if you're never able to put a dime of your own money in. This represents free money — so take it.

The next chapter will offer a unique suggestion for relatives who want to get a child within their family started down the path to financial freedom. This suggestion is a gift idea that will be more useful than many of the usual trinkets that end up in our landfills.

19

THE ULTIMATE BABY SHOWER GIFT!

"If evolution really works, how come mothers only have two hands"

▓ **Milton Berle**

The history of the "baby shower" is an interesting one. Apparently "showering" of the mother-to-be has been popular in many countries for hundreds of years — but the gifts were given after the baby was born (usually at the baby's christening). Historically it was not common to have visitors at the house until the baby was at least a month old because of the possibility of diseases. The gifts given were usually practical and mostly handmade.

Many things have changed with regards to baby showers, but "showering" the new mother with gifts is still a central element. Clothes, clothes, and more clothes — that's the most common baby shower present according to what I found on the internet. One parent lamented that their new bundle of joy would have been the best-dressed baby on the planet, if he had needed newborn clothes for longer than he would fit into them. The next common gift is toys — which in many cases has limited value for parents-to-be.

Now many sentimentalists would not like my next suggestion, but I'll make it anyway. Do you know what I think would be the ultimate baby shower gift — a gift that would offer lasting value for the baby — something that would still benefit them after decades? Here it is....one share certificate of one of the stocks I mentioned in section I. The cost could be less than $100, but it would provide enduring value. If that amount is a little out of your budget, you could pool your resources with another person and get the process started.

When I was a kid I occasionally received money as a gift. Sometimes I would spend some of it, but often I would save it. I put it in the bank. That's great for teaching the idea of saving, but how about taking it a step further an actually investing in something that grows over time. Instead of sticking money in a lousy bank account earning less than 1%, invest it in something that will pay an average of 8–10% per year. By giving this gift, they'll also become part owner in a company and be entitled to all the benefits bestowed on shareholders.

Many people buy their children (or grandchildren) Canada savings bonds. Once again that's a nice idea, but why not put your money where the rich people put their money? The rich people don't buy Canada Savings Bonds because they're not that great a deal. The rich people own companies! Ownership is where it's at! That's not to say the child will become mega-rich, but what better way to start than by owning your first share before your first month of life?

We've already covered the steps necessary in getting the first share earlier in the book, but another interesting way to give a share gift is to buy one through Oneshare, Frame-a-stock, or GiveAShare. The idea is that it is partly fun and also practical. You pay for the share and also some additional fees (usually around $150) and received a nicely framed share certificate that can be displayed. The recipient can now see their share and know that they are indeed an owner of whatever company you have purchased for them. A lot of people like this option to get kids interested in investing.

As an example, suppose you bought a child shares in Hershey. While "trick or treating", you can explain how all those acquired chocolate bars were bought by the people handing them out. These purchases added to Hershey's profit. This money was used to pay dividends — which is reinvested to purchase more shares through a DRIP. Talk about having your chocolate and eating it too! There are countless companies for which you can get a framed share. These online "one framed share" companies have a list of which shares you can buy and how much it costs — mostly US companies.

You can also sometimes buy a Canadian company as long as it's interlisted (listed on both the US market and Canadian market). Many of the largest Canadian stocks have this arrangement. However, most of the "fun" investment candidates are US companies. I mean let's face it, what's more interesting — owning shares in a chocolate company or owning shares in a boring old bank or utility company? I'd rather invest in Canadian companies because the dividends are taxed more favourably — but you have to gauge how effective an explanation that will be to a kid.

Before you go ahead and purchase shares, contact the investor relations department or transfer agent of the company you are thinking of investing in. Make sure they: only require 1 share to enrol in the DRIP/OCP (optional cash payment plan), allow small contributions and don't levy punitive fees. In addition, make sure there are no problems with foreign minor children owning shares.

Once you've bought the share, the parents can enrol the baby in the company DRIP such that each dividend the company pays will be used to purchase more shares. On Christmases or Birthdays, instead of buying crummy bonds, money can be sent to the company through the SPP to buy even more shares. The only cost is the price of an envelope and stamp.

As children get older and start to work part-time, they can also choose to send some of their money to their company to buy more shares. Gradually over time, they can see the progress of *their* company. They can see the statements of how they've gradually bought more shares. They can begin to understand how proper investing works — it's not a casino, but a steady path to wealth accumulation. A regular contribution plan can be set up such that the whole thing becomes automatic — buy more shares at regular intervals regardless of the ups and downs of the market.

So here's my thinking — you can buy a mother-to-be more clothes or toys, or you can give a gift that will have a much more lasting effect.

20

THE BALL IS IN YOUR COURT....

"Small deeds done are better than great deeds planned."
■ **Peter Marshall**

When starting *anything* new, the whole process might seem difficult. Taking the first step is always the most difficult — the most intimidating. However, once that first step is taken, the walk towards your goal starts. The old expression, "A job begun is a job half done" rings true.

In this book I've explained exactly what you can do to either set yourself or your children on the automatic journey to financial freedom.

The aim of this book is to free you from needing an extensive amount of investment knowledge or huge sums of money to get started. I've shown you some companies that I would invest in and precisely how to set the whole strategy up. Once you've followed these directions, your accumulation of wealth should become automatic.

In addition, by giving you examples of which companies you could buy and also showing you how to avoid the usual fees and commissions that are levied, you can expect a reasonable return with a relatively low level of risk.

This book lays a solid foundation for you to embark on a path of systematic wealth accumulation. How much you decide to contribute on a regular basis is your decision. You can start by contributing $1/day or even less. If you're more ambitious, you can invest more — it's all totally under your control.

As for the time you have to create your wealth — that's also under your control. Basically, the earlier you start — the better. So don't simply put this book away and forget about the whole thing — take action! For as little as $50, you can get started. The whole process is right here for you. It simply can't be any easier. The ball is now in your court!

Appendix

An Update from

"STOP WORKING:
Here's How You Can!"

"Money can't buy you happiness but it does bring you a more pleasant form of misery."

■ **Spike Milligan**

This chapter will not be applicable to you if you are following the strategy I've outlined in this book about starting to invest with a small amount of money and no investment knowledge — so feel free to skip it. It was written for those who have read my first book, but still had some questions. I hope this chapter helps answer them.

A few common questions emerged after I my first book came out. Here they are:

1. How do you know you're Canada's "Youngest" Retiree?
2. How can you call yourself retired when you're making money writing books?
3. How much did you have when you retired and how much do you have now?

4. Isn't it risky to rely on dividend income? What if companies cut their dividends?

5. What was your exact portfolio when you retired and what changes have you made since then.

Here I'm going to try to answer these questions. First of all, I didn't know if I was Canada's "Youngest" retiree — and this was excluding people who had inherited their money, won a lottery, or had achieved retirement in some other way that other people couldn't replicate. It's been three years and nobody has come forward to say that they've retired younger. Even if someone did — it's not that important. The point I was trying to make was that my investment strategy would allow people to retire years earlier than they've been led to believe — and it was a strategy most people could follow.

With the second point, I have to concede that I guess I am working — but it's by choice. When I originally wrote my first book, I thought it would be a few month project and I'd move onto something else, but it took off. I enjoy it and can choose if and when to work or not. While I'm still young I'd rather use my new free time productively rather than watching TV 24/7.

It is true that I made money by writing and publishing my first book. However, the reality of the book business in Canada is that the vast majority of books don't sell more than a few hundred copies and they lose money. For many authors, it's simply a labour of love — and that was what I expected when I wrote my first book. I was surprised and of course ecstatic that my book became a national best-seller, but that was not my original plan. My portfolio provides me with all the money I need to live on.

One of the surprising questions I keep getting is, "What is the value of your portfolio?" I guess it's reasonable as people want to have a guide for how much they should save, but I have to balance that with a desire for some degree of privacy. I think the key to financial freedom is to build up an income that flows to you automatically. The regular advice of needing *at least* $1 million was definitely not necessary for me — and shouldn't be for most people. When I stopped working, I didn't even have half that amount. Since then, my portfolio has grown, but it's *nowhere close* to $1 million. I have had an opportunity to speak to many interesting people. A few of them have revealed to me that they had over $1 million in their port-folios, but still didn't feel they had enough to stop working.

I suppose the amount you need depends on the lifestyle you want. We live in a fairly large 4-bedroom, 4-bathroom home, but we feel with a family of six, we need the space. I would like to buy a new vehicle at least every four or five years — right now we have a Toyota Sienna. I would like to go on a vacation every winter (we usually go to Florida) and also be able to take smaller trips during the summer. I like being able to eat out a couple of times a week and also being able to afford a few activities like hockey, soccer, and a fam-ily membership at the local recreation center. Basically, it's pretty middle-class. I've decided that beyond this comfort zone, more money is not dramatically going to improve my life. My time is more much more valuable — that's why I don't go off to work every day.

As far as risk goes, I'd say it's minimal. Sure it's possible that one of my companies could run into trouble and cut their dividend. However, with a portfolio of companies that sell products or services that are essential, the risk of many or all of them cutting their dividends is very remote. I would argue that working for any one of these large companies is *more* risky as many companies lay off workers even when they're making profits. The duty of the management of these companies rests more with shareholders than with workers. So having an income from *many different companies* would be *less risky* than working for *just one employer*.

My biggest risk is the income not being able to keep pace with the rising cost of living over time. These companies offer products and services whose prices rise over time. I would expect the distributions from the income trusts to rise as fast as inflation while the stocks should raise their dividends even faster than inflation over time. That's why I find long-term bonds risky — their payments don't rise over time, so you're actually losing purchasing power. For example, if you have a $100 bond that pays 5%, you'd be earning $5/year — which might buy 5 coffees at Tim Horton's if they're $1 each (with tax). Ten years from now, the price of a coffee might be $2 each, so even though you're still earning $5/year from your bond (guaranteed), you now can only buy two and a half coffees. That's why I think bonds are risky and I don't own any.

I'll give a basic outline of my portfolio when I retired and also list any changes I've made since then. I don't want to list exact share amounts (for some degree of privacy), but I'll list how much each holding represented within my portfolio when I retired (in percentage terms)

Here's the breakdown:

Algonquin Power Income Fund (APF.un)	8%
Canadian Oil Sands Trust (COS.un)	11%
Corby Distilleries (CDLa)	6%
Enbridge Income Fund (ENF.un)	6%
Encana Corp (ECA)	7%
IAT Air Cargo (ACF.un)	2%
Johnson and Johnson (JNJ)	10%
Livingston International (LIV.un)	5%
Manulife Financial (MFC)	7%
Pembina Pipeline (PIF.un)	3%
Pengrowth Energy (PGF.un)	8%
Retirement Residence REIT (RRR.un)	3%
Riocan REIT (REI.un)	5%
Rothmans (ROC)	6%
Sun Gro (GRO.un)	2%
TransCanada Power (TLP.un)	4%
George Weston (WN)	7%

Since I stopped working, I've made some changes to my portfolio. Here they are:

<u>Deletions from Portfolio</u>

IAT Air Cargo
Retirement Residence REIT
Rothmans
Sun Gro

When I was getting close to my goal of never working for a paycheque again, I took a short cut and reached for yield with some companies that weren't as stable with their distributions — which was a mistake on my part. Remember, risk is the worst four-letter word you can think of when it comes to investing. When you ignore risk, many other four-letter words arise! I would have been better off to use the money I invested here to buy a little more of the pipelines and utilities, even if they paid a slightly lower yield.

I bought IAT Air Cargo which leases out space along the runway at a few airports in western Canada (mostly Vancouver). With Asian economies growing quickly and Vancouver Airport being Canada's gateway to Asia, I figured this company would benefit from increased traffic. I didn't foresee 9/11 and the subsequent troubles with airlines which caused this company to cut distributions.

Retirement Residence REIT is an operator of retirement homes. Demographically, this seemed like a good bet with the number of older seniors increasing, but it too cut its distribution.

When I bought Sun Gro which sells peat moss and fertilizer, my thinking was that it was recession-proof and fairly resistant to competition (as peat moss is cheap enough that shipping it here would be too expensive). It also cut its distribution.

These three holdings represented about only 7% of my portfolio. I held onto them for a few years and with the distributions I received during that time minus share price declines, the end result was a 0% gain or loss.

I covered my purchase of Rothmans in my last book, but I got nervous when a court ruled that provinces could sue to recover medical costs — the risk had increased so I decided to sell. With my original purchase at $23/share and my sale of these shares at an average price of $45.50, my total gain was a little over 100% in less than two years (with the dividends). Normally I like to buy and hold forever, but in this case I sold because of increased risks.

Additions to Portfolio

Consumers' Waterheater
Pfizer
Royal Bank of Canada
Wal-Mart

I covered the purchase of Consumers' Waterheater earlier in this book. I bought Pfizer and Wal-Mart because large US stocks were cheap and the Canadian Dollar had risen to around 90 cents (which made cross border stock shopping cheaper). These are both on the dividend aristocrats list and should keep raising their dividends over time. Here's an article from mid-2006 where I wrote about investing in US stocks:

> *Massive budget deficits. An enormous balance of payments deficit. A dropping currency. We're talking about the US economy and the drooping US dollar right?*
>
> *No!*
>
> *This was Canada a little over a decade ago. "The world was coming to an end" for us. Productivity lagged. Unemployment remained high. Pessimism prevailed. The "Loonie" gradually sank eventually reaching all-time lows. American and foreign stocks were the place to be. Canada was destined to become a "northern banana republic."*
>
> *Contrast that to today. We're the only G7 country with both a budget surplus and trade surplus. Inflation is low. Interest rates are low. Unemployment is at 30-year lows. Taxes are being reduced. The world demands what we have to sell — oil, metals, resources. The "Loonie" is soaring while the "Greenback" falls. After falling to below 62 cents only a few short years ago, the currency has rebounded to its current level of over 90 cents. It has not been this high since 1978.*
>
> *The general trend of the dollar has also been reflected in the performance of stock markets. The TSX has continued to*

climb. It was trading below 6,000 in late 2002, but now sits well above 12,000. The Dow meanwhile, although trading higher than the TSX for over a decade, now sits around 11,000. I'm not a follower of indexes, but this paints a picture of the general performance of stock markets.

I retired at 34 by buying mostly Canadian stocks and income trusts and relying solely on the dividends. While many investors were focusing on new technologies and internet companies, I was buying the most boring companies — pipelines, utilities, banks. I like dividends. They help me sleep well at night. They allow me to eat — paying for my retired life. They come to me regardless of the ups and downs of the market. They're reliable.

For anyone who has read my book, "Stop Working: Here's How You Can!" you'll note that I advocated focusing on great Canadian dividend payers. To retire, simply ignore the irrational ups and downs of the market and collect your ever-increasing (tax-preferred) Canadian dividends. This strategy has worked very well. Royal Bank increased their payout 13% a few months ago. Manulife sweetened theirs by over 16%. Encana upped theirs. Canadian Oil Sands has raised theirs from $2 to $4 to $6 (a 300% gain — all within the last year).

This has been good for investors who like these stable (some say boring) dividend-payers. However, even though I'm not a huge proponent of over diversification, I would also not stick all my eggs in the same basket. With the mighty Canadian dollar and the lacklustre price appreciation of reliable blue-chip US stocks over the last couple of years, I feel we are getting to a point where a little cross-border shopping might allow one to add a few US dividend-payers to their income stream.

I know that many readers have read the doom and gloom reports about the US economy. Massive budget and trade deficits, unfunded liabilities, and an expensive war on terror coupled with the emergence of many new workers in competing countries who are willing to work harder, longer, and for a lot less money. Really, what's to like about the US right now.

Basically — not much!

This is why it is becoming more affordable for Canadians to buy small pieces of wonderful businesses below the 49th parallel. There's also a lot of industries that are so strong in the US but almost non-existent here. Major wide-moat consumer brands and pharmaceuticals come to mind. We really don't have a Coca-Cola, Proctor and Gamble, Johnson and Johnson, or Pfizer up here. There are just so many wonderful businesses to choose from, all of them raising their dividends, year after year.

But what if the US dollar keeps falling? What if the value really crashes? Isn't that what many of the economists are calling for?

I am not an economist so I won't pretend to be one. The first law of economics states, "The only thing more dangerous than an economist is an amateur economist.", so you don't need my predictions on where things are headed. I am not saying I have the slightest idea what will happen to the US dollar or the economy, so I will stick to what I do know.

I know the US is still the world's economic giant. It dominates the list of the world's biggest multinational companies. Standard and Poor's compiles a list of dividend aristocrats (companies that have increased their dividends for 25 consecutive years or more). I would recommend looking at this list (just Google "dividend aristocrats") and find companies that have large international operations earning foreign currency income which would provide protection in the event of continued US dollar weakness. With these companies you'll get a nice raise every year while you watch their international business grow as China, India, and all the usual suspects march onto the global economic stage and buy the products these companies sell. As much as I love investing in Canadian stocks (mostly because of the dividend tax credit), I can't think of any Canadian company that would make it onto the list of dividend aristocrats. Many raise their dividends regularly — but not as consistently as the aristocracy!

For example, the few companies I listed above — Coca Cola, Proctor and Gamble, Johnson and Johnson, and Pfizer have raised their dividends for 44, 50, 44, and 39 consecutive years! In other words, each and every one of them has been increasing their annual dividend payments since before I was born! That means during the Vietnam War, the 1970's oil embargo, multiple recessions, the Cold War, inflation, rising interest rates..... through this and many other events, the dividends kept marching relentlessly up! In addition, this is just years of consecutive dividend increases! The aristocrats have even more years of consecutive uninterrupted dividend payments. For example, Proctor and Gamble from above has been paying uninterrupted dividends since 1890 — before anyone alive in the world today was born!

Ten years ago Canada looked destined to become the "banana republic of the north" with a Canadian peso. Cries of linking up to the US buck with "dollarization" went out. Now we're hearing about the imminent demise of the US dollar and economy......

I'll be buying some of these dividend aristocrats (with large international operations earning foreign currency) and tucking them away while I count the dividends to rolling in. I'll let you know in ten years how it all worked out.

In the case of Royal Bank, its share price had become cheap because its US expansion plans were not going well. It has since fixed these problems. Its dividend history was covered in my first book — so I won't repeat it here.

One final question a lot of people were wondering is if I would have enough income to stay retired. They felt that inflation would force me back to work at some point. Aside from the holdings I sold (shown above), here's the performance of my portfolio as it relates to percentage dividend increases since I stopped working almost three years ago:

Algonquin Power Income Fund (APF.un)   **no change**
Canadian Oil Sands Trust (COS.un)   300%
Corby Distilleries (CDLa)   10%
Enbridge Income Fund (ENF.un)   11%
Encana Corp (ECA)   300%
Johnson and Johnson   32%
Livingston International (LIV.un)   28%
Manulife Financial (MFC)   54%
Pembina Pipeline (PIF.un)   10%
Pengrowth Energy (PGF.un)   14%
Riocan REIT (REI.un)   10%
TransCanada Power (TLP.un)   **no change**
George Weston (WN)   **no change**

Note Corby paid a *special dividend* of $1.50 per share (equivalent
to $6.00 before the 4for1 stock split) in early 2007.

In addition, all four of the new additions to my portfolio
have raised their payouts since I've purchased them. Canadian Oil Sands and Encana have benefited from a big run-up
in oil and gas prices over the last few years. I would not
expect the same performance going forward, but the payouts
are low enough that they should be sustained at their new
higher levels. Overall portfolio income has increased over
20% since I stopped working and has soundly beaten inflation over that time period.

I hope this chapter helps answer some of the questions
many readers had.

Happy investing.

Could someone you know benefit from reading
The Lazy Investor
It makes the perfect gift for any occasion.

Order using PayPal at:
www.stopworking.ca

Order toll-free at:
1-888-686-7867

$19.95 • FREE shipping!
We accept **Visa**, **MasterCard** and **American Express**!

Gift Package Set:

Both:

The Lazy Investor
STOP WORKING: Here's How <u>You</u> Can!

Only $34.95 • FREE shipping!

Quantity Discounts:

Quantity	Price/Copy
1	$19.95
2-4	$17.95
5-9	$15.95
10-19	$13.95
20-50	$11.95
Over 50	$ 9.95

**All Quantity Discount prices also include FREE shipping!